Rebel Without Applause

'Don't mention the word "English" to me.'*

'What's so horrible about McEnroe? All he does is complain. Does he kill anyone?' *Ilye Nastase*

'Despite what you read, he's a nice guy.' *Bjorn Borg*

'You're the pits of the world.'*

'McEnroe is a stiletto. He just slices people up.' *Arthur Ashe*

'Connors is an animal, Borg is a machine, McEnroe is an artist.' *David Benjamin, Princeton University coach*

'You're a disgrace to mankind.'*

'He's still my child.' *Kay McEnroe*

'Don't be a baby.' *Jimmy Connors*

'Are you in the human race?'*

* John McEnroe

Ian Adams

John McEnroe

Rebel Without Applause

CORGI BOOKS
A DIVISION OF TRANSWORLD PUBLISHERS LTD

JOHN McENROE
A CORGI BOOK 0 552 11978 4

First publication in Great Britain
PRINTING HISTORY
Corgi edition published 1982

This book is set in 10/11 pt Times

Corgi Books are published by
Transworld Publishers Ltd.,
Century House, 61–63 Uxbridge Road,
Ealing, London W5 5SA
Made and printed in Great Britain by
Cox & Wyman Ltd, Reading

CONTENTS

For EMHJ

1

REBEL WITHOUT APPLAUSE

Okay, I make faces*

Let's put it this way. I'd rather get some attention than no attention*

I do try to have manners. I'm really working on them, not swearing and all that. Maybe I'm not succeeding so well*

I guess I always had too much Irish*

It's not luck. I worked for this. I deserve it*

People keep saying I'm nastier than Nastase but I don't copy him. I don't aim to annoy people, I just can't help getting mad with myself*

Are you in the human race?* [to a spectator]

You're a cheater* [to the umpire, in the same match]

Everyone wants the crowd on their side*

He's worse than me and Connors put together
  Ilie Nastase

I die. Sometimes I just *die*   *Kay McEnroe*

He's shy   *Stacy Margolin*

You can't expect an old umpire to pick up a fast serve as well as a younger person. The average age is probably sixty. I mean it's absurd*

Altogether he looks like a baby gorilla hanging around waiting for action   *Cathy Couzens*

The game is littered with inconsistencies   *Barry Newcombe, New Standard*

The poison that this intense and intolerable New Yorker has poured into the game has spread   *Nigel Clark, Daily Mail*

McEnroe v Connors seemed to be a perfect example of the boxer v puncher analogy   *Rex Bellamy*   The Times

I have never been fined for anything obscene*

Sometimes I think he's off his nut   *Sir Brian Burnett, Wimbledon Chairman*

I have lots of interesting things to say. I just don't want to say them in public*

I don't blame John. It's time the officials cleaned up their act *Pancho Gonzales*

Despite what you read, he's a nice guy   *Bjorn Borg*

I'm emotional and he's not. People like to see that contrast*

* *John McEnroe*

He's known as the brat, but there is another extreme.

> *I thought of Chatterton, the mar-*
> *vellous boy,*
> *The sleepless soul, that perished*
> *in his pride;*
> • • • • • •• • • • • •• • • • •
> *We poets in our youth begin in*
> *gladness;*
> *But thereof comes in the end de-*
> *spondancy and madness.*

The first thing to establish here is that the connection between William Wordsworth's Chatterton and John Patrick McEnroe is a fanciful one and fragile indeed, principally because Thomas Chatterton, so far as we know did not play tennis and was a fraud, while John McEnroe does and is not. Most people, anyway, would think he was dignified by the label *enfant terrible*, let alone Wordsworth's phrase. In the 1981 Benson and Hedges final at Wembley, McEnroe might whimsically have been said to perish in his pride and there has, in his youth, been much despondancy and madness. However we have yet to see much evidence of gladness in his person or his play. At twenty-three he is no longer a kid. McEnroe was, though, a marvellous boy when he first played in Britain and absurd as such an analogy may seem to others I have, virtually from that first sensational Wimbledon in 1977, found myself thinking of him as such.

Don't make me act like a man when I feel like a boy, a lyric from a song by Daryl Hall and John Oates may be more appropriately applied to rock fan McEnroe. As may be deduced at once, this is a partial book. Essentially I like McEnroe, both as a masterly tennis player and, so far as it is possible to guess, as a person. He has undoubtedly deserved some of the vilification that has been heaped upon him. He is clearly short-tempered and hot-headed and I do not feel that excuses should be made for some of his remarks or much of his behaviour. But I do feel that the fact of his youth has been overlooked when the judgements have been made, that the scandals have been exaggerated and that the quality of his tennis has been all but forgotten in some of the furores that have surrounded him. That fingers have been wagged too much and explanations sought too seldom. The pressures that are imposed by the mixture of hostility and professional demands would have tried the endurance of most people, let alone a teenager unused to public attention and extreme stress. It has become self-perpetuating: crowds might now feel cheated if they were denied a few ragings and dramas from a McEnroe match. It is possible that, sensing the dislike he has bred, McEnroe's temper—always on the shortest of fuses—is the more easily ignited. Result: spectator disgust and outrage, further tension and injudicious rantings from McEnroe and, very probably, game set and match to the Brat.

It would be foolish to oversimplify: aggression is certainly part of McEnroe's game. Just as boxers frequently say that to command the 'hunger' they need to win the big fight they have to psych themselves into a state of rage and hatred for their opponent, McEnroe appears to thrive on the goading and a charged atmosphere. His serve is certainly like a sideways southpaw. He can usually turn discomfort of an opponent or waves of dislike against himself to his own advantage. He is intelligent enough to know that this is all part of his game and arguably to utilise, to some extent, the distaste that so often floods down the banks of spectators towards him.

Perhaps if he was an Olympic athlete his events would be Throwing the Tantrum or Jumping to Conclusions. But if it's foolish to suggest that McEnroe is perfect it is also foolish to overlook that he is a tennis player, not a diplomat. The people who complain that they paid good money to watch tennis, and not spatting between a competitor and a linesman are unlikely, honestly, to feel they have been cheated of good tennis after a McEnroe match. As his father has said, even in the most strife-ridden matches the time spent bickering may only amount to five minutes spread over four hours. Over and above every criticism that McEnroe receives is the fact that almost invariably he will give the crowd a display of magnificent tennis. And that, surely, is what they came for?

As Ilie Nastase has said, 'What's so horrible about McEnroe? All he does is complain. Does he kill people?' He is a young man who has proved to be consummately good at his sport and rather bad at holding his tongue. Sometimes he has good reason to rant and rail, sometimes not. Someone more confident, someone with a more cosmetic personality might well be able to bite the lip. McEnroe seems unable to do so and I believe that with tennis players, as with all people that one takes interest in, one should accept the bad with the good. McEnroe is human (and more to the point, since this does not seem to apply to all humans); he frequently displays vehement signs of life. It is possible that without the rough edges there would be less devastating tennis. It is also possible that given a few years McEnroe will, like Jimmy Connors and to some extent Nastase, grow out of his hooligan image. In five years time there may be another young shaver with a loose tongue, a truculent manner and a magnificent serve. By then McEnroe may have mellowed or seem mellow by comparison both with the newcomer and with his old self. There's plenty of time for the combative streak to be mined out. Personally I shall be sorry when it goes for good.

The media have been given a platinum-edged, heaven-sent contrast in Bjorn Borg and McEnroe. One is steely and utterly composed—a perfect stylist with, on court, the emotional range of an African violet. The other is equally stunning in his play but volatile and nobody's nice guy. Heroes and villains. Perfect. The contrast, real as it is, has been relentlessly milked and even exaggerated by excess attention to McEnroe's tantrums and to his wariness of journalists. While it would be untrue to say that the excellence of his game has been underplayed, it sometimes seems that this is merely a platform for less relevant publicity.

McEnroe is not of the Italian-suited, sharp-shod, chic and sharks-tooth international playboy tennis circuit. It is difficult to imagine him at ease in the jet-set, night-clubbing, discovating milieu that many of his fellow professionals are said to enjoy. A well-heeled hooligan, perhaps, but no athletic wastrel. He guards his private life zealously and, wounded by his critics and angrily deflecting what he sees as press prying, is the more misunderstood. Some people say he's a nice guy. Borg is one of them. I'd like to give him the benefit of the doubt. And even if he is as black as he has consistently been painted he's still given millions of us hours of spell-binding tennis and managed to do so despite the massed invective of much of the tennis-watching and commentating world. Some people would have caved in, but the cussedness that draws the criticism, and maybe the crowds, may have protected him too. McEnroe is no longer a lad, but as long as the 'brat' image sticks, perhaps the other extreme —the marvellous boy—should be considered once in a while.

McEnroe, it has been noted, is widely unpopular at home in America as well as abroad. 'Superbrat' is a mainly British epithet. Back home he tends to be called Mac the Mouth, Mac the Knife or The Incredible Sulk. No doubt from Toronto to Frejus, from Tokyo to Rotterdam local wags have devised similarly amusing nick names. But a particular tension seems to exist between McEnroe and British tennis fans—an extreme, self-perpetuating mistrust which is, when you stop to consider it, a little odd in some ways.

McEnroe actually displays many of the qualities that the British traditionally demand of their heroes. He is obstinate (*dogged*), aggressive (*manly*), (*modest*) he never brags about successes or makes cocky predictions, he takes issue with authority (*courage in the face of might*), and of course, he wins. This last is quite important. It's not known if he's kind to animals. One might have thought that the Bulldog Drummond and Dunkirk spirit (*fighting back in the face of disaster*) he displays could endear him to the British, but no. The British have always liked their heroes to have a quiet, unassuming charm, too. McEnroe is the strong, noisy type. If only he showed more teeth and smiles to crowds he might be seen as a sort of Flashman of the Centre Court. Naughty but nice and devastatingly effective. But he does take it all so seriously; and pukka heroes aren't allowed to admit that they're trying. If Nastase's charm had had less of the playboy and ritzy hooligan about it and if his tennis had been a shade more consistent the English would have warmed to him.

Even so, he has never been so roundly persecuted as McEnroe.

Mac has none of the social ease and grace which is called charm but which is frequently a slick and well-rehearsed pose. He says he despises phonies and I guess, then, that he is wary of people who display obvious charm since such folk are often duplicitous. His looks, domestic arrangements (until recently), and the awkward manner might once have been given the benefit of the doubt and called 'shyness', could have helped him to slip into an acceptable 'kid next door' slot. But he's no Andy Hardy. He's too sure-footed, too impetuous, too fine a tennis player and too flawed a person for that.

Perhaps the truth is that the chap who shoots down three Messerschmitts before breakfast, bales out into the English Channel, swims home to take the vital wicket in the Test match at Lords, nips off to a sponsored tap-dance show and raises £1000 for sick horses and then pops home to change and take a nice girl out to dinner, is too potent and enduring an English fantasy. Everyone knows that these are comic-strip heroes, but Roy of the Rovers and Raffles survive as national prototypes. Orwell wrote about it all at some length, and Wimbledon, as an institution, can be slotted quite easily into some of his theories about class, institutions and heroes in Britain.

It's worth remembering the great Pancho Gonzales. Now a pro at Caesars Palace in Las Vegas, ten years ago Gonzales was still prone to controversy in his championship matches. As recently as 1972, at Queens Club in London he took exception to what he considered poor line-judging. After a number of complaints he demanded that the line judge be changed. The umpire refused, so Gonzales simply walked off the court and out of the match. He said recently amidst generally reproving remarks about McEnroe, 'I don't blame John. It's time the officials cleaned up their act.'

The English have often had trouble with wayward geniuses if they overstepped. As George Best became steadily more unruly, his game declined and rightly or wrongly a link was seen here. Such a connection scarcely applies to McEnroe. Dennis Lillee and John Snow, both bad-boy fast bowlers, were given a metaphorical smacked botty with one hand and a congratulatory pat on the back while they took wickets and liberties by turns. A more recent British sporting bad-boy, Ian Botham (whose behaviour off the cricket field has not always attracted the friendliest publicity), suffered a huge slump in popularity during his troubled captaincy of the MCC tour of the West Indies in 1980-81. When, however, under the captaincy of Mike Brearey he was pivotal in England's astonishing run of Test triumphs against Australia in the summer of 1981 all was forgiven and forgotten and he became a national hero once more—a sort of combination of Garth and Harry Wharton. Botham came in for sustained criticism when he wasn't successful but was welcomed back to the public and journalistic breast when he came up trumps.

I have a suspicion that were McEnroe British—and it has been known for people from these Isles to display flashes of temper—his faults would sometimes be indulged, his cussedness admired and his victories become a source of national pride.

The English have gone off social upstarts, too. In troubled times and a recession they are less welcoming towards the unconventional. The 1960s was the tolerant time for street kids to rise. Despite his comfortable middle-class background Mac has been branded as an Irish hooligan, a New York punk who could do with a come-uppance.

If he really wants popularity here, McEnroe will have to bite the lip against the hasty remark, even if he's certain that he's right. He'll have to be nice to the spectators and wave happily after a match even if they've cheered his errors. He'll have to learn that sometimes he's wrong and also accept that officials are human and fallible too. He'll have to let a British player take a set off him once in a while, and say 'Charlie played like a dream. He really had me worried.' Learn some common sense, maybe.

But common sense can't always be applied by the uncommon person. If the price of a brisk course in charm and diplomacy was to be a decline in McEnroe's tennis and a distortion of the honesty he presents both within and without the game, I'd just as soon he didn't sign on.

2

SERVICE WITHOUT A SMILE

Come and do the same in my backyard*

McEnroe never gives up until the last point
  Bjorn Borg

They always wanted Borg to win. You'd think
that after four wins he'd let up and forget it*

If the two of us could keep lifting our games
then it didn't matter if there were a few bad
calls. It was the match that counted*

I'm a fighter*

It was the best match I ever played and lost but
I'd like just once to play great with a guy who
brings you to that level, and win 10-8 in the
fifth. That would be something*

John doesn't have any weaknesses. He has
reached parity with Connors and myself now.
Most of the big titles will be between us
  Bjorn Borg

Don't ever mention the word 'English' to me*

Wimbledon should tear up its grass*

Women shouldn't umpire in men's matches.
It's just harder to get upset with a lady in the
chair*

Lady, do you know how many serves you've
missed? Do you know how many serves you've
missed this *set*. You're sick, lady*

Don't start anything. I'm telling you, shut your
mouth, son   *Jimmy Connors*

New Yorkers are a tough crowd*

I have the right to query any decision I think is
wrong*

He will be one of the all time greats—better
than Borg or Connors   *Arthur Ashe*

The madder John gets the more Borg will like
it   *Arthur Ashe*

The match at Wimbledon was a kind of new
start. I still showed my emotion but it wasn't
bad. It was natural and the people liked it*

I don't really get down. I try to ride with the
punches*

* *John McEnroe*

Just before Wimbledon 1980 the persistent ankle injury
and its related cock-ups came home to roost. At the French
Open, after playing week in and week out all year, the injury
trouble that had been threatening McEnroe's game caused
decisive, if infuriating, action. Or rather rest. Mac admits
that he uses routine circuit matches as other players use court

practice. In fact together, to some extent, with doubles matches, his regular tournament play constitues training for his major singles games. He'd rather listen to rock music when he's not actually competing.

McEnroe was the last person to make excuses for his dismal performance in the French Open. Later he saw it rather philosophically, as a blessing in disguise, that he was knocked out by Australian Paul McNamee. It had been a great match, hum-dinging tie-breaks in every set, but the resultant defeat lead McEnroe to lay up, take it easy and get really fit before Wimbledon and his fourth assault on Mount Borg.

'I had been playing too much tennis. You can't play that much and be ready to pick your game up. You sure can't be ready against Borg, the way he picks his spots and then gets ready.' I doubt if McEnroe was referring to Borg's skin condition here.

So he rested. The green grass of Wimbledon was waiting as was the purple prose of some of the pundits. No sooner had he arrived than the latest accusation broke. Spitting. Because he'd reputedly spat occasionally during matches, this now became his most widely publicised habit. It's certainly a fairly disgusting thing to do, but nowhere was it ever substantiated that spitting had become McEnroe's new hobby. One incident was, however, picked up and discussed to the extent that, fitting neatly into McEnroe's punky image, one might have supposed that every court on which he played was boggy with his saliva and that spectators wore plastic macs on the sunniest days to avoid being drenched.

In the potted biographies of seeds given in the *Sunday Times* that year McEnroe, seeded No. 2 was said to have a vicious discus thrower's service, unique touch on ground strokes and volleys and brash confidence amongst his strengths. Weaknesses enumerated included a dislike for top-spin, fragile concentration and niggling. Watch out, the paper said, for displays of nasty temper and a unique, racket-dangling stop-volley. The combination of flare-ups and unconventional shots summarised what crowds had come to expect from McEnroe.

Wimbledon began with its usual late June fanfare and

cloudburst. The 1980 championships were worse hit by bad weather than average and many matches had to be carried over from one day to the next, and on fine days play sometimes began at the unconventionally early hour of noon. McEnroe's progress was smooth in the first round but he hit trouble in his next match against 25 year-old Terry Rocavert of Australia. To the enormous surprise of almost everyone, McEnroe had to work exceptionally hard to stay in the championships and his match with the unseeded Rocavert went to five sets. Having raced to the ground in a cab after the car arranged by the Wimbledon authorities had failed to show up, Rocavert played a sensational match and almost caused a classic upset. McEnroe, playing a slow and uninspired game lost the first set 4-6 but scraped home with the second at 7-5. After recovering to take a 5-2 lead in the third, he lost concentration and the Australian took the tie-break by seven points to four. The next tie-break proved decisive and McEnroe squared the match when he took it 7-3. The early stages of the last set were also close but McEnroe rallied and pulled away to take it 6-2.

The match had lasted three and a half hours. Too close a shave for anyone in the second round let alone the No. 2 seed, and McEnroe was going to have to play far better than this to beat Tom Okker, sometime US Open finalist, in the last thirty-two.

Three easy pieces, or rather two effortless sets and a tie-break in the middle. The 6-0, 7-6, 6-1 result took McEnroe through to his next match with South African Kevin Curren. This was another straight sets win, but as the 7-5, 7-6, 7-6 scoreline shows, it was no walkover. McEnroe only broke Curren's serve once in the first two sets. Oddly, for one whose serve is generally considered a match-winner and whose backhand is not considered classic, it was a backhand return off a second service that gave Mac the big point in the third tie-break. In a match that had been staged over two days because of continuing foul Wimbledon weather, one cheerful distraction was a curious dance McEnroe performed towards the end, with a bee. He swatted that with his backhand, too. Compared to McEnroe's slow, unravelling service which can last up to ten seconds, Curren's serve is swift and almost as accurate. Playing then at his first Wimbledon, he was tipped as a player to watch in future.

Into the quarter-finals and a match against doubles partner Peter Fleming who was beyond the singles second round for the first time. Obviously knowing Fleming's game backwards helped McEnroe and he took the match easily. The semi-final draw produced a classic clash of the titans with the two American heavy-weights, Connors and McEnroe, weighing in again.

It was a match of some drama—spun out by the lengthy pauses between games and the slow serve of both men. Thus each time it accelerated into base line and rally play—which was frequently—there seemed to have been almost a contrived build-up. Further distractions came from Connors' many breaks to spray some pain-freezing matter on his knee. There was an early fracas with the umpire when McEnroe was warned after contesting a service decision—an incident which Connors exploited to the full by wagging his finger at McEnroe and advising him to keep his mouth shut. Three games later in the first set Connors again endeared himself to spectators by making stagey asides while waiting for McEnroe to serve. The match was highly charged and graced with a series of amazing, blazing rallies and almost every point was hard fought although the scoreline suggests otherwise.

After Connors had taken the first set there was high drama in the second when McEnroe, 4-2 down, broke back. In a game which lasted sixteen minutes McEnroe had eight break points, but Connors kept clinging on. Finally Mac took the game and roared through the rest of the set to take it 6-3. Hindered by a service that wasn't quite equal to McEnroe's, Connors battled on. He had two break points in the last game of the third set but was thwarted by McEnroe's touch and anticipation. A break down in the fourth set, McEnroe was in some trouble but the pressure worked its curious osmosis on him and he soared back, put Connors on the run and took the set 6-4. The final score read 6-3, 3-6, 6-3, 6-4.

Perhaps the extent to which this game taxed him contributed, later that day, to a defeat in the semi-finals of the doubles. He and Fleming went out 6-3, 6-2, 6-3 to the Australians McNamara and McNamee. But in a sense this might have been a good thing. It meant that McEnroe could be single-minded in his approach to the match that had seemed to be a foregone conclusion since that first extraordinary summer of 1977. A confrontation with Bjorn Borg in the Wimbledon final.

The curious thing was that this match was treated almost as if it was the first time these men had ever met on court. They had, in fact, played several times since 1978 when McEnroe had beaten Borg in the semi-final of the Swedish Open in Stockholm. Some of their matches had been widely reported. But so steeped in mythology and kudos is Wimbledon that they might just as well have, by a series of accidents or arranged destinies, delayed their confrontation until now. It had all the makings of an epic, all the sense of destiny of King Kong and Godzilla and all the potential for a cliffhanger as Sherlock Holmes' encounter with Professor Moriarty at the Reichenbach Falls.

Magically, Saturday July 5th was a sunny day. I was furious. I couldn't watch the match and cursed myself about some stupid garden party I'd agreed to go to some weeks earlier. All the way there I was figuring a way of getting home again without accidentally seeing, hearing or otherwise discovering the result of the match before it would be relayed in irritatingly abbreviated form—unless it had been a three set walkover—on television later that evening. It wasn't even a private party, more of a function, so I didn't entertain the possibility that there might be a television to watch if I could swing it. But miraculously, inside one of the fustian rooms of the university building in whose grounds the party was taking place, there was a small colour television. I switched it on guiltily but at 2 pm wandered back outside since the match was late starting. Tracy Austin and her brother had been taking an unusually long time to win the mixed doubles final.

I muttered something about it being a shame about the tennis to one of my fellow minglers. We exchanged glances and glided indoors. It's always easier to be naughty if there's someone to share the blame. Settling uneasily into armchairs we decided to watch the first few games and then to operate a shift system. Fifteen minutes on, fifteen minutes off and briefly filling each other in on the state of play at our changeovers. The trouble was that Mac won the first set so easily that I couldn't bear to get up. It didn't matter. Within an hour two-thirds of the party guests had given up in the garden and were crowding around the screen and squabbling for chairs and floor space. There, as at Wimbledon, there was a loud majority of Borg support but a small division of McEnroe shock-troops. As the match ground on and the empty bottles accumulated, the audience participation rose above the level of appreciative gasp and murmur and became gloriously, sometimes violently and occasionally hilariously unsubtle. Cheers and booze. Outside the sun shone brightly and the remaining guests locked intellectual antlers on Wittgenstein or brown rice and the Third World. The pallid ones indoors saw a match that might never anywhere, between any two people, ever be bettered.

Quite why it is such a classic has been debated. No-one denies that it is, but the match began slowly and until the third set the tennis was variable. It was the fusion of occasion, place, its long countdown, its length, the intensity of the struggle and the contrasting natures of the two combatants that made it resemble a five act Shakespearean drama. Someone called it 'a symphony of a thousand points.'

Seventeen minutes after two o'clock Borg and McEnroe walked onto the Centre Court. There were loud cheers and some incredibly bad-mannered boos. The match began in extraordinary fashion with Borg looking shakey and double-faulting twice in his first service game. John roared away with the first set 6-1 in just twenty-seven minutes. It seemed too good to be true: could he win? If so, would he please slow down a bit and let Borg win just a few more games to make it more exciting for us. Ludicrous thoughts. McEnroe was in the match immediately and was so overwhelming, especially in his serve, that the two of them looked mismatched. An unsettled and tentative Borg won only seven points against McEnroe's serve that set.

The match took shape and balance in the second set with Borg still having trouble with his serve but beginning to fling some cross-court shots which even McEnroe's speed couldn't reach. Games went with service until the ninth when McEnroe had three break points for a 5-4 lead and it looked then as if he'd have two clear sets on the board in a minute or two. Borg served very deep into the corner, raced to the net and fired off winning volleys that saved the game. Then, always a service break up since the beginning of the set, he only had to break through in the twelfth game tie-break to take the set 7-5. They had been playing for a further forty-nine minutes.

Both men, a set apiece, were making fewer unforced errors. Borg had the advantage again of opening the set so it only took a break in the second game to give him a daunting lead. Soon he was 4-1 up despite double-faulting twice in the fifth game. Two games later Mac almost broke back but Borg deflected a total of five break points, snatched back the game and with a 5-2 lead needed only to hold service once more to move into a comfortable two sets to one lead. Now it was McEnroe who looked like a slightly uncomfortable guest at someone else's party. A little tired, too, perhaps, having played two strenuous matches the day before—with Connors, and the doubles final—whereas Borg had had all Friday to rest and prepare. He approached the fourth set aware, along with 14,001 other people around Centre Court that he had to win it to stay in the match.

This time he served first and the heroic fourth set was underway. With his commanding position Borg was now totally at ease on court but Mac's determination was ascending. Neither man gave an inch. Almost every point was closely fought and the rallies that occured in virtually every game were each a series of elegant and scorching strokes. Surer than ever of his service McEnroe was composed, grim-faced and unhurried as he survived two early match points. Then he pulled back, crippling Borg's service and at six games apiece there had to be a tie-break.

Some tie-breaks take little longer than a conventional service game. It can be won with as few as seven points. Seven shots even. This one took twenty-two minutes—just five minutes less than the whole first set—and thirty four points were played. During the course of those minutes, possibly the most gripping, nerve-jangling interlude of any game of tennis ever watched, Borg had five championship points and McEnroe seven set points.

By the nature of the tie-break, the 'sudden death' play

off introduced to Wimbledon in 1971, it is a theatre of the game where service power is incredibly important. That McEnroe can often serve his way out of a tight corner, that he usually thrives during tie-breaks is well observed. But his temperament would not seem to be ideally suited to the stress and pressures built into any match-deciding tie-break, let alone the desperation-stakes significance of this one. That he won it says much about his psychological strength and maturity. No panic, no lapse of concentration. Instead, a steely, gritty, obstinate calm to match Borg's natural cool.

There was crisis after crisis. One moment the championship was within Borg's grasp and the next McEnroe had snatched it away by inches. The length and power of the rallies was testimony to the nerve and ferocity of each player. McEnroe lunges towards a backhand cross court from Borg, unplayable against anyone else. He stretches out, you can hear him gasp and you see him drop a forehand volley over the net into an empty court. The first matchpoint is saved.

Borg wins the 6-6 point with a whiplash backhand. To save the match's fourth matchpoint, the second of the break, McEnroe shoots a risky backhand right down the line. The chalk powders up but it's in. Somehow Borg reaches it. It looks like curtains for Mac but the ball glances the net and bounces back. The backhand was unreturnable after all. A forehand winner from Borg makes it 8-all. And so it went on, minute after minute, the title falling time and time again into Borg's palm but slipping through his fingers. Altogether McEnroe had seven set points and Borg pulled six of them back. Borg had five championship points and McEnroe pulled them all back. On his seventh set point McEnroe's service finally decided the set and the boy was back in the match.

After such a Herculean endeavour it was little short of miraculous that the final set was no anti-climax. Nerves now a little frayed, Borg served two double faults before scraping through to take the opening game. He soon steadied and the old raging pattern was quickly re-established.

Somehow, however, it seemed that the force of the set was something that Borg was fighting *with* and McEnroe *against*. He did not give in until the last point and the

23

tightness of play, quality and inventiveness of cross-court returns and lobs was sustained till the end but at 7-6 in the fifth long set Borg fired a magnificent double-handed backhand and the match, and for the fifth time the title, was his. 1-6, 7-5, 6-3, 6-7, 8-6. The match had lasted almost four hours and Borg won twenty seven games, McEnroe twenty six. Of the 373 points Borg had taken 178 and McEnroe, ironically, 195. There is not likely to be a closer final for some time.

Borg was on his knees and kissing the bald brown turf. McEnroe was stretched on his back, still flailing from the effort to reach the shot that finished him. Only the Centre Court crowd was on its feet. The applause was just about worthy of the match and almost half of it was for the loser. Throughout the game McEnroe had displayed total grace. For a while, at least, he was forgiven. I went back into the garden and did some sulking for him.

Presentations. Cup born aloft. Shaking hands, nods of acknowledgment, one broad smile and one brief flicker. A crowd of photographers. Many poses and grins from one man and one long stare at the lense and a drink from the machine from the other before he tucked the rackets under his arm and made the tired trudge back to the shower. The side that wins the Cup Final bounds up Wembley's steps to shake the royal hand after ninety minutes or more on the field while the losers seem barely able to lift their calves for the climb. It doesn't always seem quite fair, even if the result was well-earned. Borg deserved to win but John didn't deserve to lose.

Borg had quite a lot to say afterwards and so did McEnroe's critics. Even Mac himself eventually broke out of monosyllables to describe it.

'I gained more satisfaction from winning a match like this than from an easy one. It was the best match I have played at Wimbledon so far. I kept telling myself not to get tight or nervous,' said Borg. Those of us who'd been rooting for McEnroe in the university library had been both. 'Like Connors, McEnroe never gives up until the last point. It's not going to sink in till tomorrow that I have won my fifth title. It was exhausting out there, not physically but mentally. My ambition is to be remembered as the greatest player of all time,' he went on. Modest, huh? 'It was not only the toughest of all my five finals, it was one of the toughest matches of my career,' he added.

McEnroe was already thinking ahead to the US Open at Flushing Meadow. 'Come and do the same in my backyard,' he said.

The magnificent match that McEnroe had played won him a new and unfamiliar range of adjectives from the press. Indomitable, courageous, glorious, entrancing, mature—that sort of thing.

Mac himself had this to say about it all. 'I am disappointed but I tried hard and it was a good match. I can't complain for I never had a break point in the fifth. I didn't get a good hand from the crowd in the beginning but eventually I felt a change of attitude. But they always wanted Borg to win. You'd think after four wins he's maybe let up and forget it but no such thing. He hits the ball harder than ever these days.' Later, back in New York he'd play videos of the final over and over again, watching to see how Borg's volleying and backhand had bettered him, studying the errors and sometimes taking delight in moments of glorious triumph. The tie-break set was run through for pure pleasure, the fifth cassette but rarely. 'Match always ends the same,' he said. Sitting eighteen inches away from a video screen he'd watch with detachment. 'Nice serve, John,' he'd say at the deflection of one match point.

Speaking to Mike Lupica he said, 'A match like that gives you something to shoot for.' Sounding rather like Holden Caulfield, McEnroe continued, 'I went for it. It was the Wimbledon final, and Borg and all but I decided I had to go for it. I don't know why somebody responds the way they do. Like I wasn't trying to hit my second serve harder than usual, or deeper, but that's the way it was turning out. I wasn't trying to hit the ball harder than usual or deeper but that's the way it was turning out. And I am proud of myself. I was out there and I was trying to lift my game the same way he was lifting his. It was unreal. He'd lift his game then I'd lift mine, then he'd lift his, then I'd lift my game again. That's what makes tennis or any sport exciting. That's why the crowd kept responding the way it did. Suddenly I realised I didn't have to worry about the crowd or the linesmen or anything. If the two of us could keep lifting our games then it didn't matter if there were going to be two or three bad calls. It was the match that counted. Bad calls; you go on. Aches and pains; you go on. I showed my emotions a couple of times and so did he but that all seemed to fit in. I learned a lot that day, about Borg, about tennis and about me.'

We all did, and we realised something that isn't always quite true in matches, even those of the highest calibre in tennis, cricket, football, boxing or darts. This match—which like all matches except those in team sports where a draw is possible—had a winner but it approximated more than most matches several of the many definitions of the word 'match'. Something that flamed and burned right until the last moment when the holder blew for the umpteenth time on his fingers and extinguished the flame. And some of the Oxford English Dictionary's definitions, too: *One's equal, one's fellow. An antagonist, rival. An appointment. To meet in combat. To ignite. Some composition that bursts into flame when rubbed on a rough or specially prepared surface. To provide with an adversary of equal power. To pit against another. To arrange in a suitable or equal pair or set.*

Talking about the tie-break McEnroe said, 'It was so quiet. I remember it being so quiet. You remember funny things, like starting to feel cramp in places I'd never cramped before, like my feet, behind my knees. I remember getting mad because I'd had to play Connors the day before. But only for a second because then me and Borg had to get on with it.

'For me that match clarified that this is what I want to be doing. You forget sometimes. There's all that money to be made, but I don't have to worry about money any more. There's more to it. And you know I can play better. That's the best I ever played in my life and *lost*. But I could have played better, I could have. It makes you realise, hope, that you can work harder and maybe win that kind of match. I'd had a pretty disappointing year up to then. I'd played too much and been hurt. Then I played that match and even

26

though I fell short I felt good. Playing that well puts the joy back into the game.

'My biggest ambition,' he said, 'is to beat Borg on clay. I want to beat him three sets out of five on clay in Paris.'

The pair had been expected to clash the following month at the Canadian Open in Toronto, but McEnroe had to drop out when, leading 4-2 in the first set of his second round match with Erik van Dillen, injuries laid him up. Maybe he was saving himself for the US Open. In any case, those who had hoped to see Borg and McEnroe fight it out for the title —as they had the previous year, when Borg won—were disappointed.

McEnroe and Borg did, however, meet a few weeks later in Mac's 'backyard'. At Flushing Meadow Borg's path to the final of the US Open—his ninth shot at the title—was more relaxed than Mac's, although he needed five sets to beat the unseeded South African Johan Kriek in the semi-final. His 4-6, 4-6, 6-1, 6-1, 6-1 win exemplifies that even after a thoroughly stiff start Borg can do an about turn and carry off a match with apparent ease. In his own semi-final against Jimmy Connors, McEnroe had a lengthy and more complex fight on his hands. The match took well over four hours and was finally decided by a seven points to three margin in the tie-break that closed the fifth set. The score was 6-4, 5-7, 0-6, 6-3, 7-6.

Had it been played in an epic, final, forum the match might well have been regarded as one of the great tussels of recent years, but all semi-finals lack the glamour of a tournament's climax even though they are often better games. So this will simply go down as one of the great 'B' movies and another notch on the scoreline of the Connors v McEnroe records. It was an amazing and unpredictable game. With one set tucked away and leading 5-4 in the second, Mac seemed primed for a quick win. Then suddenly Connors took command in a way that reminded one of Popeye's wondrous feats of strength. Perhaps Connors took spinach capsules at the changeover. At any rate he went on to win eleven games in a row, taking the second set, the third with breathtaking ease and putting himself well up in the fourth. McEnroe's scarlet headband seemed to be like the proverbial red rag to the bull. He appeared finished, although the downturn had not been without its responses from McEnroe. During the disastrous third set he'd asked for a change of umpire. The man was, said McEnroe, an idiot and a numbskull. In passing it's amusing to see what quaintly old-fashioned epithets McEnroe often uses in his rages.

His recovery was as dramatic as his catastrophic decline. There was no change of umpire, but Jim still couldn't fix it. From 1-3 down in the fourth, McEnroe stormed ahead to take the next six games. Such was his agression at this stage of the match, even though he'd hit a golden streak, that he once hurled his racket the length of the court, sending it slithering to Connors' feet. Shortly afterwards two officials strolled onto the court, informed McEnroe that he was fined $250, and wandered off. McEnroe seemed utterly unmoved by this unusual interruption and the game continued. He went on to take the set, although by now Connors was fighting back again and the fifth set was a peerless, tightly fought affair with both men pulling themselves out of exhaustion to produce noisily executed forehands and dazzling rallies. The tie-break clinched it for McEnroe.

On the same day he played another five set match—the doubles final with Peter Flemings. His day was a rewrite of the Friday before his Wimbledon final since he and Fleming were defeated: this time by Bob Lutz and Stan Smith. Ten sets of top-level tennis is some way to get into shape for your final with Borg . . .

There are two men whose achievement Bjorn Borg most wants to match or excell. In the broadest sense McEnroe isn't in it. Borg wants, like Don Budge in 1938 and Rod Laver in 1962 and 1969 to achieve the grand slam. That is to win Wimbledon, the French and US Opens and the Australian championship in the same year. Both Budge and Laver were amongst the 20,000 people watching Borg and McEnroe in their final on September 8th 1980. Having won Wimbledon and the French Open already, if Borg could win this title he could go on to Melbourne at the end of the year with three out of four under his belt. But the US Open has always jinxed Borg. Ten times now he's been defeated there, seven times by left-handers. If nothing else, the elusive US crown is likely to keep Borg playing professional tennis despite rumours that he plans to retire in 1983.

Another year he'll swing it perhaps. This year maybe? McEnroe has said he'll be surprised if Borg never wins the US Open but by threatening not to return to play there after his 1981 defeat unless arrangements were altered so that he didn't have to play under the floodlights that adversely affect his game, perhaps Borg has laid a foundation stone for withdrawing from the event and thus conceding that he has one dream that won't come true. Win some, lose some, Bjorn. Win mostly, as it happens. You never know—people might still regard you as the greatest player of all time even if you never win the US Open or achieve the grand slam. No-one's going to forget you in a hurry and when you chat to the diners at that Third Avenue restaurant in Manhatten they say you're going to open, no-one's going to take the rise out of you and say your pickled herrings are better than your backhand ever was.

One of those pictures that says everything was taken the moment the Borg-McEnroe final closed. Mac's arms are raised high, his racket grasped in his left hand. Body thrown back, euphoric eyed and mouth wide open in a huge whoop. It's a portrait of triumph and exuberance. He looks young and happy. It must have been a very sweet moment. By common consent this final did not match the pulse-racing Wimbledon clash in terms of atmosphere or standard of play, but it was a real revenge: the backyard dream come true.

'I figured if I was going to beat Borg it would have to be here on my best surface,' said McEnroe. After the match, 7-6, 6-1, 6-7, 5-7, 6-4, McEnroe spoke modestly and was already a little subdued. He did not comment on the fact that the match had, in its way, been won the hardest of ways. Psychologically it's very daunting to start a fifth set knowing you have relinquished a two-love lead after the second set, and fearing that you'll be unable to raise your game again when it seems so long since you were in front. When the other man seems to have found perfect form at the most opportune point of the match. It's harder to enter a fifth set like that than with any other permutation of sets on the scoreboard.

Borg had only had to go the full distance 13 times since 1974. No-one else had taken a fifth set from him.

The match lasted for fifty-five games—exactly the same number as the Wimbledon final—and in the first set Borg was poised to take a lead, serving twice for the set, but McEnroe pulled back and then had the nerve to save two set points in the tie-break. 'Borg gave me the first set', said McEnroe, recalling his opponent's carelessly played tenth and twelfth games. Having the opening set whisked away disturbed Borg who played with less assurance in the second and served only moderately well, whilst McEnroe was ferocious. People said Borg looked listless as the second set slipped away. The third set settled down to a level of grinding if not inspirational excellence, Borg winning by the superiority of his baseline play. Many of his shots, though, were landing in the net, and McEnroe was volleying superbly. In the fourth set, McEnroe said, he felt he was finished, that his body felt like it was falling apart, but somehow he clung on, and as Borg's service, particularly his second serve, declined by degrees especially in the final set, McEnroe's strength and spirits returned. Games went with service in the final set, until 3-3 when a combination of double-faults and ill-placed forehands gave Mac the edge. He conceded only one point in each of his remaining service games and took the match.

Speaking later of his patchy service a dejected Borg was floundering for explanations. 'Perhaps I was not tossing the ball high enough.' He had failed to hold service in the second set, double-faulted nine times during the match, served only five aces and less than half of his first serves were good. Even the famous backhand had looked less dangerous than usual.

'The Wimbledon match was much better and played at a higher level. I think John can play better than today and I think I can,' Borg added. A better game might have ensued if both players had not been so tired. The championships might be better devised with a rest day between the semis and the final. Borg would certainly have preferred it if they'd not played through dusk into darkness under floodlights. But a better result, for McEnroe, could not have been achieved and nor could the timing of it. His pleasure at retaining his US

30

Open title (won first in 1979), overcame the very slight sense that there was more glory to losing a great match than to winning a good one. However it seemed that some, in taking this latter view, were determined to withold from McEnroe full appreciation of his win even at that supreme moment of undisputed dominance. It might have been nicer for John if his victory had not been explained away by a 'below par Borg', if it had been suggested that Borg had played as well as he had been *allowed* to play. If McEnroe had been given full credit, just once. With the *Daily Telegraph* headlining its reportage** of the match with *Bold McEnroe denies Borg the Grand Slam he so richly deserves* and the same article concluding with '. . . while McEnroe started the Wimbledon final as a villain and finished it as a losing hero [I'm not sure]* he did not finish the Flushing Meadow final as a winning villain for denying Borg his just deserts', what was the poor boy to think?

That autumn McEnroe added the Australian indoor title to his list of 1980 successes by beating the holder, Vitas Gerulaitis, 6-3, 6-4, 7-5 in Sydney. It was a match marked by squabbles on both sides of the net as well as snappy tennis. Most of the arguments came as a result of line calls, the quality of which had been widely queried throughout the tournament. McEnroe and Fleming had a good day in the doubles finals, beating Tim Gullikson and Johan Kriek 4-6, 6-1, 6-2. It was just about time for the Benson and Hedges Tournament in London.

It might be unfair to describe this event as one of the lesser firework displays on the pro-circuit calendar but it doesn't come near the top of the list of prestige tournaments. However in Britain where such events are relatively scarce, it always gets plenty of attention, and coming back in 1980 to defend his title at Wembley, McEnroe truly was star of his own show. Borg's agents do not permit him to play here

* I.A.
** *by Lance Tingay*

except at Wimbledon so his absence was no surprise, but the eagerly awaited clash between Connors and Mac was stymied because Jimmy's mother Gloria was unwell and he stayed home. It was the likes of the Mayer brothers, Sandy and Gene, Stan Smith and Harold Solomon that McEnroe was pitted against this year.

His course to the final included encounters with Solomon (whom he'd beaten in the final in 1979), and Rick Meyer. In the final he met New Yorker Gene Mayer and took him apart 6-4, 6-3, 6-3. This was McEnroe's fifteenth consecutive win in the B&H competition. In three years he had dropped just one set. After a rough start, with Mayer leading 3-1, Mac's more versatile and resourceful play, speed and marvellously angled shots forged through. The match lasted less than two hours and McEnroe popped £15,000 into his pocket afterwards. He and Fleming won the doubles, too, beating Scanlon and Teltscher 7-5, 6-3.

Possibly his most dramatic match of the tournament was a mud-slinger with spectator Mrs. Betty Albone of Dunstable, Bedfordshire. Millions of television viewers saw her take issue with him during his semi-final with Solomon. Sitting in the third row with a friend, Mrs. Albone gave McEnroe a piece of her mind when he had shouted at her for applauding a double fault. Play was delayed by two minutes while McEnroe enquired who the hell she thought she was. As good as you, Mrs. Albone replied. After a warning from the umpire, McEnroe resumed play despite of or because of Mrs. Albone's comments that people paid their money to watch tennis, not bad temper. Afterwards, Mrs. Albone said she thought she might have made a bit of a spectacle of herself but that many people had applauded her outburst.

On his twenty-second birthday in February 1981 McEnroe collected his largest wage packet ever—the £60,000 first prize in the Pepsi Grand Slam at Boca Baton, Florida. While defeating Guillermo Vilas 6-7, 6-4, 6-0 in just over three hours he had failed to overcome the hostility of the 11,000 spectators. Even though McEnroe once over-ruled a line judge to get a decision reversed in favour of Vilas, amidst the routine slammings of racket in self-directed anger he was, as usual, playing without much support. The slow clay court favoured the Argentinian's top-spin ground strokes and McEnroe adapted his game to play with less ruthless ferocity. There were splendid rallies, but at first this change of tactic affected McEnroe's game. At one point, set up and leading 3-1 in the second, Vilas seemed to have the fat cheque within his grasp but then McEnroe began to dominate and a tired Vilas could not respond. After much dashing and rushing McEnroe evened the match and took the third set, after two and a half hours, with almost casual ease.

In May 1981 McEnroe joined Rosewall and Connors as the only players to win the WCT (World Championship of Tennis) series for the second time. A nice little fillip before Wimbledon. He'd beaten Johan Kriek 6-1, 6-2, 6-4 in the Dallas final. Aside from an entry in the record book and the £45,000 that McEnroe took home with him it was not a notable match. Generally regarded, in fact, as the least interesting final since the WCT series began in 1971, Kriek did little that day to emulate the style and spirit that had taken him to the final. McEnroe, thus, had little need to display much of his range.

The old-stagers final, however, played between Ken Rosewall and John Newcombe, was said to be a thing of beauty—a match with artistry and excitement. Rosewall, after teetering two points away from defeat beat Newcombe 4-6, 7-6, 6-4.

Maybe there are another five years ahead during which Borg will meet McEnroe in some resort or capital every few months. Maybe they will go on at top pro level considerably longer than that: McEnroe is twenty-three now and Borg only twenty-five. Stan Smith, after all, is still doing the rounds and he's well into his mid-thirties. Not winning many, but taking part. There may be something just a tiny bit undignified, faintly funny or faintly sad about the veterans matches. Somehow it's different with doubles. It's no-one's business but their own but in a sense I hope this circus palls for McEnroe—and Borg too for that matter—before they start to become the tennis playing counterparts of Muhammad Ali or Gary Glitter: one comeback too many.

3

MY OWN BACKYARD

He's still my child   *Kay McEnroe*

John is a perfectly normal teenager except in one thing . . . the way he plays tennis *John McEnroe Sr.*

Every kid wants to be a rock and roll star, and I still do*

He believes its phoney not to show how you feel   *Mary Carillo*

I find it very hard to relax on court. I was brought up to be serious*

He's no star at home, just one of my three sons   *Kay McEnroe*

He was funny and witty and he'd try almost any prank   *A schoolmate*

He was such a jerk we were glad to see the back of him   *A different schoolmate*

He was a terror   *Former coach*

McEnroe's notion that he is always right is
straight out of *Camelot*   *Sandy Mayer*

Kids imitate us in everything we do. It's a big re-
sponsibility   *Gene Mayer*

We are not stage parents forever pushing the
kids on   *John McEnroe Sr.*

She hates watching me* [*of his mother*]

All our kids got the same instructions. Play
your best. Don't quit. But we want you to be gentlemen   *John McEnroe Sr.*

He's always had drive since he was a little fellow, always had to be first   *Kay McEnroe*

You could always hear John's matches from
blocks away. Sometimes he cried when things
went wrong   *Mary Carillo*

John and his father are so similar. The volume
goes up about ten decibels if they disagree on
something   *Stacy Margolin*

* John McEnroe

John Patrick McEnroe ws born on February 16th 1959,
in Wiesbaden, West Germany, where his father, a lieutenant
in the United States Air Force was serving as a personnel
officer. His paternal grandparents came from County Cavan
and County Westmeath in Southern Ireland and McEnroe has
indulged, along with many others, in the speculation that his
hasty temper can be traced back to the old sod. It's a
picturesque supposition and there's likely to be a little truth in
it, but it's usually a mistake to draw on national caricature for
character analysis. People can be hot-headed in any language
and from any sort of soil.

Perhaps it's worth a quick glance at his horoscopes.
McEnroe's birthday is near the cusp of the sign of Aquarius.
Individuality, independence, strong opinions and a stubborn
streak are said to be the dominant characteristics of the sign.

Aquarians are also said to have a fascinating glamour, magnetic powers of attraction and kind hearts.

A look at the Chinese horoscope is more interesting. Along with all other people born between February 8th 1959 and 27th January 1960, McEnroe comes under the sign of the Boar. Gallant, sturdy and courageous, it says, boar people apply themselves to a task and see it through. They may not seem to be smooth but they are honest, natural and pure gold beneath a tough exterior. But boars are also said to be keen on universal harmony, loath to carry grudges, lenient, patient and unassuming . . .

Boars are supposed to be their own worst enemies and to have trouble with self-control, to have extraordinary stamina and to be passionate. But they are also meant to be good at making and keeping friends and to be prone to allow others to take advantage.

Despite such speculations, a quick glimpse at family life and childhood are more likely to shed light on the complexities of McEnroe's character. His mother, Kay, was a nurse before marriage and family life took over. She and John McEnroe Sr. have two other sons, Mark, who is three years younger than John and a full-time student at Stanford University and scruffy young Patrick who is now fifteen and has been tipped to become a tennis player in the same league as his big brother sometime towards the end of the 1980s. A slight, pretty, fair-haired woman, Kay McEnroe organised John's cheque book and finances during the early professional years and has said firmly that John, like all her sons, had a routine, disciplined childhood. In fact she said that they were, if anything, stricter with John than with the younger boys. Emphatically the McEnroe children were not brought up to be self-seeking.

'We are not like stage parents, forever pushing the children forward,' said Kay McEnroe a few years back when public attention was first focussed on her eldest son.

In any case, McEnroe has continued to regard the family home in Manor Road, Douglastown in the New York suburb of Queens as a haven of familiarity and comfortable normality, even though he has property of his own in Manhattan and

The family.   (Photo: Graham Wood/Associated Newspapers Ltd)

Florida. 'At home he's just one of my three sons,' said Kay McEnroe.

The support and protection that McEnroe received from his parents, particularly in the early years of his hurtling rise to fame and notoriety, lead him to say that it gave him an edge that left him free to concentrate totally on his tennis. John McEnroe Sr. continues to be a stabilising and supportive influence, managing as he does his son's career and helping him with many of his decisions. Kay still does his washing for him although John has left home.

Douglastown, where the family moved when John was one year old after McEnroe Sr.'s spell in the forces, is a comfortable, leafy, middle-class residential neighbourhood. It was, perhaps, a trifle inconvenient for John when he was commuting as a teenager to Manhattan's exclusive Trinity School (the oldest royally chartered school in the country), as he was often away from 7 am to 7 pm, having taken part in school sports activities after classes. But the very thought of this quiet, prosperous district and the McEnroe's pleasantly gabled home should dismiss any lingering notions that McEnroe is a sharp little New York street hustler who prowls the tennis arenas of the world for prey and survival.

John McEnroe Sr. played serious basketball at college. After leaving the airforce he worked in advertising for the J. Walter Thompson agency in New York before studying law at Fordham University. Now, at 50, he works for a prestigious Park Avenue law firm, (specialising in corporation law, mergers and stocks), and closely guards his son's financial and professional interests. He claims he is not a Svengali figure. McEnroe tends to travel alone to his tennis commitments around the world and Superdad will join him for important matches. Unlike Bjorn Borg who is seldom seen without his coach, Lennart Bergelin, and Marianna Borg as well, McEnroe is something of a lone star. He and his long-standing girlfriend Stacy Margolin (who also plays tennis professionally) sometimes arrange for their respective schedules to collide geographically, but they by no means make a regular point of it. Tony Palofox, McEnroe's coach, scarcely ever travels to watch his matches and while McEnroe Sr. will often defend his son against some charge or other and supervises aspects of his business dealings, he does not provide a day to day emotional prop. The strength and closeness of early family life have given McEnroe enough self-reliance not to require one and the parents insist that early lessons have essentially been followed.

'At the top of the sport the pressures are intense and you can't expect players to be automatons. But I believe Johnny tried to follow what we taught him as a child. All our kids got the same instructions when we sent them off to the courts: "Play your best. Don't quit. But we want you to be gentlemen," ' said John McEnroe Sr.

Commenting on one of his son's alleged court misdemeanors, McEnroe Sr. said, 'Sure there are times when he overdoes things, but the media can distort incidents—and that's not just a father's excuse. Johnny will always be grimacing and scowling when he means business. When he's gone further, that represents one half of one percent of the period of the entire match.'

The extent to which Superdad can be entirely unbiased about his son may be imagined from the story that when John played basketball in school the father would shout down sharp and succinctly expressed advice to the referee of the game, especially if John was picking up a red card for a 'technical foul'. Stacy Margolin said John learned his style of aggression from his father.

Douglastown, close enough to both La Guardia and John F. Kennedy airports to be highly convenient to the international player, also offers good local facilities for talented youngsters. John first learned at the local club and later had the advantage of finding a gifted mixed doubles partner, Mary Carillo with whom he was to win the mixed doubles in the French Open in 1977, living only three blocks away. These days young Patrick who is, according to his father, better than John was at the same age (although Patrick will have been playing for far longer, since a racket was thrust into his small fist at a very early age) still gets in some practice at the local courts.

John showed an early aptitude for several sports, not specialising in tennis until his teens. As a toddler he showed such an extraordinary eye and ball control (the anticipation that Bjorn Borg was later to describe as 'radar eyes') that once when the father was tossing a ball to his two-year-old son in the park, a passer-by enquired of McEnroe Sr. whether his companion was really a little boy or a gifted midget! At the age of four John first had a baby racket placed in his chubby grasp but it was not until he was eleven that serious concentration began.

The former Australian Davis Cup coach, Harry Hopman, took him into his training group at the nearby Port Washington training academy and it was here that McEnroe learned the rudiments of his serve and volley game. He was apparently already showing signs of his more boisterous side and towards the end of his years of coaching there, was suspended when, after a junior tournament in the Catskills, he was caught running down the hotel corridor with a flaming bath towel. A fuller version of this tale is that McEnroe shouted 'Fire' at 2 am, poured a bucket of water over someone who ran for help, and then set fire to the towel and was suspended (with two other boys) never to return. Ironically Harry Hopman has been among the adjudicators on the many boards and committees who have sat to consider McEnroe's appeals against his post-Wimbledon 1981 fines, but Port Washington appears to bear their wayward former pupil no hostility, and have presented him with a silver plaque to mark his tennis achievements. The academy, on Long Island, New York, is exactly the kind of place that Paul Hutchins, Britain's Davis Cup coach, would like to see here. A kind of clinic for exceptionally gifted youngsters, it is run with careful single-mindedness and aims to produce future champions. The intensity of practice, coaching and advice that it offers is one of the reasons why the United States, with its very different attitude to professionalism in sports, continues to produce young winners in field after field.

Harry Hopman told journalists long after McEnroe's days at Port Washington (but before the tribunals), about his reading of the character of his erstwhile pupil. 'Johnny is strong-willed, not brash. There's a difference. There's never been a champion who hasn't been strong-willed or determined to assert himself in his own style. Sometimes Johnny's style is blunt. He disagrees, but he is surrounded by older people—most of his opponents and officials—and he feels he must stand up for himself at times. A brash person is loutish and Johnny is not. He's a kid from New York City and I've found such youngsters will speak out.'

Mrs. McEnroe says, 'Nobody bothers to go deeper, to see the real Johnny. He's no star at home. I do cringe sometimes when he does something I don't like and it's good for him to lose sometimes. But we're not worried about him. He's growing up fine.'

American writer John Powers made cogent points when he said that the very fact that McEnroe was not the street punk he had been labelled, that he did come from a secure and loving home, that he had gone to a good school and had never been short of a dollar or two was partly what made McEnroe behave with a mixture of cockiness and truculence. The upbringing that could have turned out a perfect preppie had, in McEnroe's case, quite the opposite reaction and had instilled in him a deep suspicion of order and conventionally correct behaviour.

Young John was sent first to the Buckley County Day School but when he was older went on to the smart, conservative Trinity School in Manhattan. A classmate remembers 'He was funny and witty and he'd try almost any prank.' He took part successfully in schoolboy soccer, basketball and tennis competitions. Tory Kiam, who was No. 2 in tennis to John at school, says McEnroe was modest about his successes out of school. During those years when he was climbing in the national junior ratings he'd not speak much about some of the big tournaments where he'd emerged as a winner. Tory Kiam points out that as a young player McEnroe was already railing regularly at officials but would often do so on his opponent's behalf as well as his own, sometimes insisting that a point should be 'given back' to the other player if he did not feel he had earned it justly.

'He would win so easily in school that no-one really understood how good he was. But he'd never beat anyone love love, even when he could have. He'd let a set go to two all, for example, so as not to humilate the other guy.'

Perhaps because he was brought up strictly, he was an early rebel. Rebellious in those tiny, insignificant ways that seem like a big statement when you're fourteen. At school where attention to correct uniform was unusually strong for the United States, John wore a denim jacket instead of the regulation blazer and these days he still eschews jet-set tailor-mades. In 1979 at the ceremonial lunch in Dallas after the WCT finals, Brian Gottfried said it was one of the most remarkable occasions he had ever attended 'because John McEnroe is wearing a tie.' He can rise to the big occasion —pictured with Nancy Reagan at a White House reception for the victorious US Davis and Wightman Cup teams in September 1981, McEnroe wears a brown suit, a blue and white striped shirt and a widely flapping tie, as well as what looks like a very expensive watch. Eyes fixed in the middle distance, he looks earnest and sincere—a portrait of a young candidate, in fact. But characteristically dressed in some kind of bomber jacket and crumpled jeans, the old desire not to be typecast, to go against the respectable image, is usually still with him. Behind the bravado, however, there is a certain wistful reservation about the unpopular image that his aberrations, large and small, have brought him. After losing the final at Wimbledon in 1980, he said he figured it would take another ten such final defeats before the crowd were on his side. There's some exaggeration, some realism, some weary resignation and some pathos in a remark like that.

In many ways he still behaves like a recalcitrant child. After he had been accused of spitting at a woman spectator at Boston's smartest tennis venue, the curiously-named Longwood Cricket Club, McEnroe denied it pofaced. Then he ceded 'I spat in front of her. I never got her.' Neither the act itself, the specious denial or the final mischievous justification, irresistible though it may have been, are endearing. Childishly again perhaps, McEnroe professes to like junk food above all other kinds. It is notorious that he was out wolfing pizza with friends on the night he might have attended the formal post-Wimbledon banquet at the Savoy in 1981, and despite a wallet fat enough to enable him to ignore the right-hand side of even the most expensive and sophisticated menus, he still prefers burgers, beer and plain family food. Some of the more fattening junk has been cut out recently, resulting in weight loss of a stone and even more speed on court, but McEnroe still calls for chocolate during changeovers in matches, both for the energy it brings and, of course, the taste.

At Trinity McEnroe found time to be a good, solid, all-round academic student as well as a sports star. It sounds as if he was one of those maddening people who can diversify but still excel and remain, on the whole, well-liked by peers as well as teachers. Latin, English Literature, Spanish and Calculus have been listed amongst the subjects Mac handled with ease. His former Latin teacher, Englishman Frank Smith who comes from Stratford upon Avon, remembers that sometimes McEnroe's sports commitments interfered with desk work and after botching some test paper an anguished McEnroe yelled, 'Mr. Smith, you don't know what *pressure* I'm under!'

His old headmaster, Mr Hanly, said that McEnroe was in fact rather shy. 'That temperament is something I never saw in any respect. It only comes out when he is playing competitive tennis. He played for the school all the time and only ever got angry with himself. He had wonderful patience with some of the younger kids—terrifically supportive and helpful towards them.' Speaking of John's skills on the soccer field Mr. Hanly described him as 'our Jimmy Greaves.' Authorities at the Port Washington Academy where John went solely and specifically to improve his tennis, tend to back up the view that his agression only emerges in the heat of competition. The vice-president, talking of events that led to John's 1976 suspension (possibly the burning bath towel drama, but the vice-president did not expand), said that while he was at the academy he had displayed a volatile temper. 'John was with us from twelve years of age and up to his seventeenth birthday. He was a terror.'

Another ex-school mate recalled how when John was sixteen he flew off to take part in a tournament in Virginia, beat Charlie Pasarel, Bob Lutz and went out to Ilie Nastase in the final. But he didn't mention this in school on the following Monday morning—his friends only learned about it by reading the newspapers. This man, like others, remembers McEnroe would never humiliate a player he could easily beat in a less illustrious competition but would always allow them to take a few games away from him during the match.

Rock music continues to be important to McEnroe. In his dressing room at Queens, between matches in the Stella Artois tournament a couple of years ago, he was listening carefully to Pink Floyd tapes. He was going to a Floyd concert later that day and wanted to be primed and receptive to the music. It is known that he saw Bruce Springsteen in 1981 while he was here for Wimbledon and believed that he went straight to an Allman Brothers concert on his return from that sad post-match debacle. At home and in the house in Manor Road, there are stacks of tapes ranging from Meat Loaf and Eddie Money to Billy Joel, Fleetwood Mac, Pat Benatar and the Beatles. McEnroe will, however, remove the headphones to watch *General Hospital*: he's reported to be almost as religious about this soap opera as he is about his tennis. He also goes to the theatre occasionally, although one might venture to hope that *No Sex Please, We're British* which he saw with Stacy Margolin in London does not entirely exemplify his interest in the performing arts.

Mr. and Mrs. McEnroe are clearly and rightly proud of their son. They indulged him, no doubt, as many parents will indulge a first-born, but if this indulgence also included encouragement in the sports for which he showed such aptitude they also ensured he had the best formal education their money could buy. They were loath to see him turn professional before he had completed it. The scholarship to Stanford University in California which John had won was not, after all, to be sneezed at. But they accepted the inevitable when John's tennis pressures became greater and greater and after a year at college they did not stand in his way. Kay McEnroe said she knew John was just too talented to wait. They conceded realistically, but for some time afterwards ensured that that they personally oversaw most practical and financial aspects of his life. A combination of fondness and mutual respect seems to have endured. Certainly the warm, informal, familiar bolt-hole at Manor Road, Douglastown still provides McEnroe with the kind of unqualified acceptance that he has found difficult to achieve elsewhere and which, as the pressures of success increase, he needs as much as ever.

Maybe some of the more prosaic virtues of security rubbed off too, since in 1981 McEnroe was scrutinising art books and catalogues from the galleries with a view to investing in pictures. He must, after all, do something with all that money. Reported a year or two earlier as saying he wasn't interested in collecting jewellery ('I prefer that kind of thing as presents') he would seem to prefer to spend his loot on solid investments, not trinkets. Pictures, after all, could grace the walls of the two homes he has bought. He drives a lemon yellow Cadillac and has bought a Mercedes for his brother Mark. On paying the bills when he's out with a group of friends McEnroe will usually, but not neccessarily, pick up the tab. He doesn't like it, he says, if he feels he is being exploited. Certainly there is little surface flash about his life style and he is said to be more moved by the ten dollar bill he receives every year from his grandparents on his birthday, and by small gifts from the stalwarts who support him, than by extravagant possessions and his huge earnings.

To counter, however, the evidence that McEnroe is a kind-hearted and simple soul, deeply misunderstood, there is the report that when he was seventeen and sent off to summer camp he refused to play tennis with any of the other youngsters there because they weren't up to his standard. And another school contemporary has said, 'He was such a jerk we were glad to see the back of him.'

By 1977, the year he stunned Wimbledon by reaching the semis, John was the leading junior player in the United States and at the top of the worldwide Pepsi Cola Junior Grand Prix circuit. That year he took the great leap from the shallow junior pool to swim with the big fish at top level competition. And that year, too, he had his first brushes with journalists. Quite how his steady, generally happy childhood primed him to react to pressmen and women with such snappiness and with all the signs of someone who is deeply insecure has to be a matter for speculation. There's been plenty of time to redress matters if it was simply because he got off on the wrong foot in the first place, and anyway that first year the general attitude towards him was rather positive and encouraging. At seventeen he was still very immature and unused to public attention and pressure. He was nervous and apt to treat the inanities of some journalists with the pompousness and solemn sarcasm of extreme and precocious youth. But apart from the old yarn about volatile Irish blood flowing in the veins there is little to immediately explain his truculence.

His father is said to be combative, but I daresay Bjorn Borg's dad lost his temper now and again. Borg, in fact, has spoken of his own tendency to bad manners when he was a young teenager and how a suspension before he became well-known internationally, taught him forever to behave impeccably on court. Borg had a lapse in the Masters tournament at Madison Square Gardens in late 1980. During his match with McEnroe (which he won) he argued with the umpire and earned two penalty points.

Certainly in McEnroe's case a basic intolerance, an inability to suffer fools or what he sees as foolishness, has exacerbated things. To questions which he considers unworthy of his time he will simply turn his head away and remain mute. Such behaviour does not endear him to the ladies and gentlemen of the press who like to be treated with respect. Few press conferences can have culminated in full scale fights, as one of McEnroe's did in 1981. Journalists, so affected by the stroppy tempo of the interview took to squabbling among themselves. By the time McEnroe left a number of them were on the floor.

As a measure of the speed of McEnroe's success and of the extra strains that were imposed on him as an eighteen-year-old—pressures which would have tested the calm of the least stressful of men—six months after turning professional he had beaten more top players than anyone else on the circuit, won four grand prix singles titles, five doubles titles with Peter Fleming, spearheaded the USA's win in the Davis Cup final against Britain, qualified for the Colgate Masters tournament—and won more than £200,000. Such statistics may help to account for outbursts of stress: they don't explain why the potential for tantrums exists in the first place. The 'punk' typecasting was convenient late-seventies shorthand for any rebellious kid. Punk is a neat four letter word that looks striking in banner headlines. But did McEnroe chain his ankles together on the Centre Court? Did he eat safety pins? Did he have pink hair? Well, okay, he did spit now and again, but as a lead in character assessment, 'punk' is a non-starter.

When McEnroe went to Stanford in 1977 he was still an amateur and strong-willed enough to resist for a while the temptation to turn pro and earn a fortune in endorsements as well as prizes, something he must have been reminded of at each of the economics classes he attended. In 1978 his mother said that they'd all considered the possibility of him putting off college and going there after his peak playing years were over but decided against this as 'you can only be an eighteen-year-old freshman once'. As things worked out, the lure of the big-time—probably more in terms of tennis than money—was too strong to resist for long.

The McEnroe home is just a few blocks away from the Douglastown Club on Little Neck Bay and the family joined the club for social reasons in the first place. In a small, quiet community like Douglastown opportunities for young marrieds to meet others and for their kids to make friends are limited. No-one in the family played tennis at the time, but soon McEnroe Sr., then John and later the other boys took up the game. John's very first real racket was an old worn out bat, far too heavy for him, and discarded by a family friend. The first racket actually bought for him came from a discount store and to this day McEnroe uses a standard model rather than a hand-built, tailor-made one as most of his fellow professionals do. Aged eleven, surprising everyone, he reached the semi-finals of an under-twelves tournament and a month later, only six weeks after his first game of tennis, he won a similar competition. From that point his parents recognised that their son had exceptional talent and he began to attend Port Washington.

Kay McEnroe remembers that John, aged eleven, set off for his first national competition with his one cheap racket and, driving him to the airport, all three of them were worried about what he'd do if he lost it. They stopped at the club on the way, where Mark was on court, grabbed his racket and lentit to John as a spare. Mark, poor lad, thought he was being punished until the situation was explained. It may be completely insignificant, but of the three McEnroe boys Mark is the only one who has not shown exceptional tennis talent. Competent, certainly, but not in John's class or the league Patrick promises to enter. McEnroe Sr. says that he once overheard two kids talking about John in the early days of his junior tournaments. One remarked that he thought McEnroe was a good player, but the other one replied that he couldn't possibly be because he only had two rackets!

All the trophies that McEnroe wins, including the silver plate from Port Washington, are kept in the Douglastown home, in the living and dining rooms. Even when John was living there he didn't keep them in his own room. Mrs. McEnroe insists that he's self-deprecatory and shy. She says that the house seems quiet now that all the sons are away and it's no longer necessary to stick fingers in the ears before entering John's old room. She says it seems tidy too, just like any other mum. But amidst the plants and books in the downstairs rooms there are plenty of reminders of her eldest son's activities. Space must be running out now for the cups and trophies and for the stacks of magazines that have McEnroe's face on the cover.

In between the strict academic schedule at Trinity and classes at Port Washington McEnroe moved steadily up the junior rankings. 'John was a perfectly normal teenager except in one thing . . . the way he played tennis,' said McEnroe Sr. He travelled with the junior Davis Cup team, went in for a junior event in South America, won the Sunshine Cup, played in Dallas in the WCT juniors and entered the Pepsi circuit. By 1977 he had won the French Juniors, qualified for the Open and won his first round match. He went out next match to Phil Dent of Australia, but he had his revenge at Wimbledon soon afterwards when he beat Dent there in straight sets. At the French Open that year he and Mary Carillo—a new partnership, not the long-term buddies they have sometimes been described as—won the mixed doubles. So it was a new face but an experienced and successful boy who qualified for Wimbledon a few weeks later.

Someone who knows McEnroe's game well and has watched his progress for many years, is his coach, Tony

First entry. Wimbledon 1977.
(Photo: Norman Quicke/London Express News & Feature Services)

Palofox. Interestingly Palofox rarely travels to watch John play. The very idea of such an arrangement angered McEnroe. 'Boy, is that the easy way out. You put all the problems on him. Make the plane reservations. Do the laundry. Do this. Do that. Get the rackets. It'd make more sense for me to have a secretary.' Palofox works as head pro at the Cove Racket Club on Long Island and is a former Mexican Davis Cup player. He was John's tutor for six years, first at Port Washington and later at the Cove Racket Club.

Palofox coached a lot of kids but concentration was what put young Master McEnroe a cut and thrust above the rest. 'Like a lot of kids he'd get angry with himself when things didn't go right. Other kids were more talented but couldn't do the things Johnny could at his age because no-one could really concentrate like he did.' Palofox, who has since trained Patrick McEnroe also says that the youngest boy was better at eleven than John was, but at that age Patrick had already been playing for seven or eight years and John only a matter of weeks.

What made McEnroe choose tennis when he was a football quarterback, the baseball pitcher, the basketball high scorer and good enough at soccer for the Stanford coach to write to the McEnroe parents to see if there was any chance that their boy could join the college squad? Clearly personal preference; but why prefer one sport you're good at over all the others? Perhaps because all those other games are team sports requiring a sympathy and cohesion amongst a group of players whilst tennis is a duel. Man to man combat, rackets like rapiers and almost as arcane a language as that of fencing. Or cowboys, with pistols drawn in Main Street at high noon. Perhaps it was this lonely theatre of personal battle that drew young McEnroe to tennis, where every player is starkly at risk, where defeat or victory are personal, not shared. Where individuality makes, breaks and is scrutinised. And none more relentlessly than McEnroe's.

Superdad has pointed out that there have been games where the crowd has gasped at some display of McEnroe's pettishness while tolerating an identical stress reaction from the other guy. He says it's all because of image—people reacting to what they have been primed to watch out for.

50

'It bothers me when people say bad things about me. It doesn't seem to bother Connors,' is just one of the several contradictory things that Mac has said. On other occasions he's professed to be unwounded by criticism, but that sounds like the self-defence response of the sensitive. Other times he's said that grass was his favourite surface although he generally claims to prefer clay or artificial surfaces; that could be youthful fickleness. In any case McEnroe is paradoxical and inconsistent. He's also unpredictable—often when one might expect a match to be full of fireworks and furore he will confound everyone by behaving perfectly. Arthur Ashe, who as McEnroe's Davis Cup captain has sometimes had occasion to lecture John on his behaviour but is also a huge admirer of his game, has sometimes been held up as a model champion for John to emulate.

'I admire Arthur Ashe but I'm no Arthur Ashe,' is McEnroe's response to this. At least it's realistic. Ashe, known particularly for his calm and psychological stillness, could scarcely be more different from McEnroe and it would be impossible to imagine McEnroe effecting such a character metamorphosis.

'Tennis is big business and there's nothing very gentlemanly about that. But I don't believe I'm the same person off court as on. Deep down I'm a nice guy and I expect you to believe it.' Some might find it marginally easier to believe in fairies.

4

THE WUNDERKIND

I don't care if I don't smile on court. That's me
out there and people can take me how they
like*

Wimbledon crowds are strange. If you lose a
few matches they like you better   *Chris Evert
Lloyd*

I don't care if they make mistakes. I expect
them to make mistakes. I just want them to admit to them*   [*on officials*]

I don't know if I'll ever beat Connors but I'll follow him to the ends of the earth*

I shall have to talk to my parents about whether
to make tennis a full-time business*

I've never tolerated phoniness in anyone, and
there's a lot of it at Wimbledon*

I'd rather get some attention than no attention*

I'm shy*

He cannot abide his own imperfections or the
mistakes of *others*   *Daily Mail*

John is no longer the young upstart. He has arrived   *Jimmy Connors*

Are you in the human race?*   [*to a spectator*]

A woman shouted at me 'You're ugly'. I've
been called a baby and all sorts of names. They
may be true but it's unnecessary. It's hard
enough as it is to go out there with the crowd
against me*

We went to Speakers' Corner at Hyde Park.
John picked a fight with one of the speakers
  Mary Carillo

John borrowed a jacket and we went to the Wimbledon ball by tube   *Mary Carillo*

* *John McEnroe*

When John McEnroe made his sensational Wimbledon
debut in 1977 he really did look as if he needed his mummy
out there on the court with him. His face was characteristically set in the resolute scowl of a brave child who is lost,
frightened but determined not to cry. Pictures taken then
show him furrow-browed and scared-looking. No less aggressive than he is today but without the marks of arrogance
and contempt that years of winning, of attack and of
deflecting intrusions into privacy, that years of character
assassination and often justified criticism have made. It is a
face without scorn because until then, publicly at least, he
had not been scorned. He was, after all, just a boy.

At the time, having confounded the seeding committee
by reaching the semi-finals and having become the youngest

ever male to do so, the tennis pundits turned a benign and surprised attention towards him. He was praised for his stamina, nerve and talent. He had enormous promise; we were all assured that we'd be seeing and hearing more of this fine young man.

I was lost from the start. That year it was, perhaps, fair to saddle him with names like 'potato face' and 'sulk'. Later leanness has rendered the first, at least, ridiculous. But then he was indeed slightly puffy-faced and chubby-thighed. His shorts looked a size too small—it seemed a minor miracle that he could squeeze a tennis ball into the pocket during service games. The red band round his forehead and the apparent squint made it look as if he had a bad headache much of the time. No athlete's symmetry or graceful bone-structure then. Just a kid who looked as if he'd wandered out on court by mistake, whose thick neck and faintly portly body and whose air of bewilderment made you wince a bit. Until he tossed the ball slowly upwards and served. Then you just gasped, along with his opponent, the crowd and McEnroe himself. Then as now, he appeared to take little pleasure in his points and victories.

But it wouldn't have mattered much to me if he'd been hopeless as well as helpless-looking. Although he might have endeared himself early on to the Wimbledon crowd and the British tennis-watcher, right then in 1977, if he'd had the decency to lose cheerfully and win generously, it was all the same to me. I'm glad he wins, but I'd have watched out for him every Wimbledon in any case, just as I always watched out for Nikki Pilic from Jugoslavia who had a few good years in the late sixties. He never did anything much after that but he always had me fiddling with the dial to watch his match rather than the big one on the Centre Court just because for some reason I liked him. That first year I liked McEnroe's mad spiky hair and his defensive truculence. This was partly because it seemed clear at once that McEnroe was not out to co-operate with the Wimbledon crowd.

Go to a Test match, sit almost anywhere and you will become almost immediately aware of both a sense of generosity and knowledgeability amongst the spectators around you. There are of course exceptions, but at an international cricket tournament the crowd will usually know that if runs are not being scored it is not necessarily because the batting is poor but because the bowling and fielding is excellent. A good stop will be applauded as will be a fine throw back to the wicket or a judiciously placed field. These will be more quietly recognised than a spectacular catch or a perfect over, perhaps, but the crowd is likely to understand the subtleties which prevent a racing run rate. They will also enthusiastically cheer the skills and triumphs of the side they did not come to support. It would be wrong to generalise about tennis, but Wimbledon is singular, and here at any rate, spectator response seems to be a little different.

The Wimbledon crowd tends to regard itself in the highest possible esteem. It almost seems to clap itself for being there, to designate itself as a kind of jury. Different factions will applaud the mistakes of the opposition, including unforced errors and double faults. Most of all it is banked in a daunting array of real or assumed middle-class 'respectability'. Crowd behaviour there, however, reminds me often of comedy sketch images of debates in the House of Commons. Much rowdy shouting for 'order'. The crowd at Wimbledon demands obedience, a smiling loser and, perhaps more than anything else since it can no longer hope for an English victor, it demands respect for itself. Amidst the thousands there who behave like this, of course many are both knowledgeable and restrained. But the collective 'feel' of the crowd is one of refined aggression (rather like the atmosphere on the first day of the January sales at a good department store), peppered with sanctimoniousness and ignorance.

It's like a theatre audience that is flattered by a clever showbiz performer who tells the jokes, makes the asides and creates an artificial common ground of shared references. The audience feels comfortable and when it claps part of the applause is directed at itself for being there, for understanding the double-entendres. Wimbledon audiences like the players to give them what they expect. They like to be acknowledged, they like to be thanked for appreciating the tennis. They find it rather churlish if someone who has just sweated off five or six pounds in a three hour match won't thank them with a smile afterwards. They feel insulted, demeaned, even.

It's quite easily understood. For years people in Britain have known that even if these islands can't any longer produce a player like Fred Perry, even if we have dreadful economic problems and the Empire's gone away, even if it rains every day for the entire fortnight, Wimbledon is still the greatest tennis tournament in the world. It has become one of the undisputed remaining national status symbols. As Arthur Ashe observed, profaning Wimbledon is like profaning the Queen.

It's probably true that to win Wimbledon—with its eccentric grass surface, its funny ritual of beginning play after lunch, its amateur status throwbacks and its place (archaic though this may be), in the London Season—is still to win the greatest prize in the game, even though the prize money itself is comparatively paltry. So the crowd clings on. National pride is at stake and every matron in a flowery hat has bought herself a day return ticket to an age and society when things were different. The event should be afforded the respect it deserves and young fellows who fail, apparently, to recognise the honour of being there, who won't smile or wave or say afterwards what a pleasure it's been to have had the privilege to entertain the people and take part in their glorious institution, are unlikely to be popular.

None of this would be so objectionable if the audience, or such a large part of it, were not so frequently sanctimonious and rude. Ignoring downright ignorance for a moment, it is ill mannered to hiss and boo a player as he enters the court, to cheer as he makes a mistake and to attempt to distract him at a tense moment. McEnroe has consistently endured such treatment at Wimbledon so it is perhaps not surprising that exhausted after many matches and feeling, possibly, that the crowd have had their money's worth, that he has failed to be charming afterwards. All this, in Wimbledon terms, amounts to the unforgiveable: not only does he win (sometimes in itself considered somewhat vulgar) but he fails to be nice, awed or humble afterwards.

It is curious how Wimbledon, often satirised as a place that exemplifies some of the most absurd of English suburban manners and pretensions, should come into its own for two weeks every year. Become the focus of world sporting attention. If McEnroe was English and fully aware of the class nuance embedded in both the bricks and mortar of the houses in Wimbledon's leafy roads, as well as the significance it has as a national institution, he might be better able to understand the reception he gets and the press he is given. Tennis and the summer would be badly impoverished without Wimbledon, but it has a nasty side and just as it takes any visitor a while to understand a new environment I guess it will be some time before McEnroe sees some of the less superficial reasons why he has been so unpopular there. His own behaviour and Wimbledon's traditions are classic oil and water. By the time things are clearer to him he may, like Jimmy Connors, have become an old rogue of the tennis establishment. I hope not.

In 1977 John McEnroe was ranked 270th or lower in the world ratings. He'd come to England to play in Junior Wimbledon, took part in the qualifying round for the championship proper in Roehampton and, having won three preliminary matches, was faced with the dilemma of playing in the junior competition where he was top-seeded or taking a chance in the main event. He opted for the latter but maintained his amateur status and his winnings from Wimbledon that year—about £4000—were channelled back to the American Tennis Association. While Vitas and Jimmy and Bjorn arrived at the All England Club in chauffeur-driven Bentleys or Rolls, John McEnroe travelled to the ground by tube train and bus, clutching his kit bag and rackets as he stood with the tournament ticket holders in the over-crowded carriages of London's District Line. Between matches he rubber-necked round London with Mary Carillo.

The media build-up was slowish. But by the time the *wunderkind* was facing a semi-final match with Jimmy Connors the full glare of publicity had McEnroe squinting. The quarter final victory over Phil Dent had paved the way for a massive curiosity about this odd newcomer. McEnroe said he thought he'd drop dead if he won that match against Connors at Centenary Wimbledon—his first on the Centre Court. Three months younger than Rosewall had been when he first reached the semis in 1954, McEnroe was clearly as excited and thrilled as he was pressurised by the occasion. His father flew in from New York to watch his boy, albeit in a rather less vocal parental spirit than that of Gloria Connors whose encouragement, admonishments and advice to Jimmy from the VIP box had in recent years become one more Wimbledon tradition.

The No. 2 seed and the 1000-1 outsider had never met before, on court or off and although McEnroe lost it proved to be a pivotal moment of his career. Earlier McEnroe Sr. had followed John's progress by telephone and expressed regret that he couldn't be there to watch: now he became personally involved. John, winner of junior tournaments at Dallas, Rome and Paris was still planning to study full-time, had no notions of beating Borg and spoke like a hero-worshipping kid about his admiration for Rod Laver. Until now he hadn't seemed to be taking Wimbledon or a tennis career quite seriously. He was sanguine but not awed.

'I hope they keep me back here all the time,' he'd said after an easy victory over Sandy Mayer on one of Wimbledon's rather shabby hinterland courts and before the quarter final with Dent. He seemed to be the last person to take his tennis future for granted. 'I came here expecting to be lucky to take two games a set and I can't, even now, say I feel one of the guys on the circuit. I shall have to talk to my parents. Right now I'm just happy to be playing well,' he said before the Connors match. But he added, with a flash of things to come, that he had no intention of being daunted or overwhelmed by the weight of the occasion. 'I don't let Wimbledon or the opposition intimidate me. That's the way to lose matches.' He also said he thought he'd have the crowd behind him and for once he was probably right.

That summer was certainly the first and probably the last time he could bask in our national propensity for sympathy for the underdog and while he was regarded as something of a curiosity he definitely wasn't disliked. The papers were describing him as 'engaging.' Connors, on the other hand,

(A) Sensational victory. McEnroe beats Tim Gulliksen (US) in the Stockholm Open Tournament, 1978.

(Keystone Press Agency)

(B) The Champion takes a break during the finals.

(Keystone Press Agency)

was still the big bad boy of the game and as 1974 champion did not endear himself to the Wimbledon crowd by failing to take part in the Centenary parade of living champions. Marriage, fatherhood, a new line in court manners and a new menace of tennis have done much to improve his public image.

The semi-final posed problems of protocol for the officials. As a junior and unseeded qualifying Mac had been assigned to the lowliest of Wimbledon's changing rooms but for his big match with Connors he was allowed to move up to swankier quarters assigned to seeded players. Despite a few references to contested calls, to mild reprimands for unspecified expletives and an early dubbing as 'this fiery youngster', Mac's outbursts had not attracted vilification and were explained away as the result of high tension and youthful spirits. Never before and seldom again has McEnroe's behaviour been partially attributed to stress, youth or other mitigating circumstances. In those days he could mutter 'stupid linesman' after a dubious call and still have the loss of his next two games against Phil Dent in the quarter final attributed sympathetically to dejection and tiredness. On the whole, when he went out to meet Connors, people both in the crowd and in the press would have been rather pleased if he'd won.

Mac had had a share of luck to reach the semis. The two top seeds in his side of the draw had been eliminated early on so he had to face neither the muscle-bound power of Italian Andriano Panatta or the ruthless serve of Roscoe Tanner. In 1979 Tanner roared back to form and with a new curly perm and a run of splendid matches reached the final with Borg. That year he was known as 'the man from Lookout Mountain'—a more picturesque nickname than McEnroe has ever collected. In his first match John had beaten the Egyptian Ismael El Shafei, then Rhodesian Colin Dowdeswell (each in three sets), the German Karl Meiler (in four), before triumphing over Sandy Mayer 7-5, 4-6, 3-3, 6-1. This was the first of a series of matches in which McEnroe has had the measure of Mayer and over the years the other man has been more critical and outspoken than any of McEnroe's other victims. In the quarter final match with Phil Dent, seeded thirteenth, fortunes swayed from game to game over the full five sets and being the fight it was, it was the first match that attracted a real furore of attention.

McEnroe had appeared to have trouble fighting successive waves of depression but in retrospect perhaps the way these were scrutinised and reported merely reflects the public's lack of familiarity with his unsmiling concentration. He started grimly and each game went with service until the seventh—McEnroe often looking like breaking through but being frustrated at deuce. However, a tremendous backhand pass gave McEnroe the break at last and he went on to take the first set 6-3. In the second set, punctuated with double faults and culminating in a tie-break, McEnroe's nerves simmered and an oath earned him a reprimand from the umpire. He lost the set 8-9. When the next set went to Dent 6-4 McEnroe clearly thought the match was slipping away but he pulled round to take the fourth set 6-3.

Taut and nervous in the fifth, McEnroe again looked as if he'd be beaten by Dent's superior mobility. But he recovered from 40-0 down in the first game and began one of the rearguard actions that have become familiar. Against the odds he took the set 6-4 and suddenly the following day's match with Connors seemed less of a formality.

'For the first time I started to feel nervous,' he said after the Dent match. It suggests the pattern we have come to expect: a kind of Dunkirk doggedness, a refusal to look defeat in the eye and a simultaneous ability to summon up reserves of energy and imagination when other players thus depressed would be hindered. McEnroe has since demonstrated that the tight corner is one of his most dangerous spots, that he runs better on empty than almost any other player and that tension ignites his game. The match with Connors was not quite a classic of this kind, but he had given us in his quarter final a sight of the apparently nerveless strength that looming defeat and real self doubt can bring to him. He often starts playing his prettiest, riskiest tennis when it looks like he has nothing to lose.

Connors beat McEnroe in four sets, 6-3, 6-3, 4-6, 6-4. The two Americans were on court for two hours and thirty-seven minutes and no-one would have called it a vintage match. Had McEnroe not taken the third it would, indeed, have seemed dullish. Connors did not play his best because he was not forced to. The adage that a team or player will perform as well as the opposition allows is countered by the fact that they also play only as well as they need to. Connors was not pushed that day.

Possibly awed by the occasion, after all, McEnroe never had much of a grip on the match. In the third set, leading 3-1 he found form briefly. Although he lost that advantage he fought back to another when he broke service in the tenth game and took the set with a marvellous backhand. But even moments of imaginative play and some close fighting at the net did not make the fourth set much more than a formality. Connors met Borg in the final the following Saturday and went down, like McEnroe in the semis, with honour intact but no prizes. The final was a five-set piece and Connors went down fighting. It was Borg's first retention of his title.

It is worth noting that despite being eliminated in the semis McEnroe won more consecutive matches at one Wimbledon than anyone since Bill Tilden in the twenties. It usually takes seven victories to win Wimbledon and take away the trophy. McEnroe won eight and left with nothing but a burgeoning reputation. It's easy to overlook the fact that he'd had to win three matches before the championships in order to play at all. Even if those Roehampton qualifiers were relatively untaxing they were, none the less, vital to his progress and each would have imposed the strains of any crucial game.

On the same day that Connors knocked Mac out of the fight the match which—until 1980—came to be thought of as the great post-war confrontation took place between Borg and Gerulaitis. It was a five-set marathon so devastating that it overshadowed the final itself. Until Borg met McEnroe in 1980 his title was never again so dangerously besieged. Gerulaitis, oddly, has never (at Wimbledon at any rate), repeated the heroics and verve which took him through over three hours of classic tennis and a fifth set tie break which decided the final score of 6-4, 3-6, 6-3, 3-6, 8-6.

'I don't know if I'll ever beat Connors, but I'll follow him to the ends of the earth.' In those days Mac saw Jimmy as the main contemporary hero. It would be some time before he even alluded to the possibility of beating Borg. June 30th 1977 was both the climax and the anti-climax of his astonishing Wimbledon debut. Many moulds had been cast: the early warnings, the firebrand image, the unsparing, no quarter court tactics. The chief precedent that year was the shuffle onto the Centre Court and if he continues playing as long as a Stan Smith, a John Newcombe or a Billie Jean King we have many more years, many more shuffles and many more five set set-tos to look forward to.

It doesn't take a genius to spot outstanding talent and in fairness, no-one claims to have 'discovered' McEnroe. He claimed attention from his first major championship because he deserved and commanded it. Few people could have been aware just how strong a force he would become, how controversial he would remain or how diversely he would entertain the public. In retrospect it's easy to spot the signs but despite the 'Superbrat' moniker and the ghastly publicity he's stirred up McEnroe has never needed or courted these attentions. And of course nobody would take much notice of him anyway if he wasn't so consummately good. He's a self-made man.

5

THE CIRCUS

Good serve, wasn't it lady? Wasn't that a nice
double fault? Did you like it? You're sick,
lady*

Too fast, too fast   *Buster Mottram*

It's ridiculous that the most important event of
the year should be played on grass*

I've heard there's some really bad stuff about
me in the English papers. It must have come
from you*   [*to John Parsons of the Daily
Mail*]

I can't say, even now, I feel like one of the
guys on the international circuit*

I can't let up and joke with the crowd, but yes,
I think I am different off court. A lot more easy
going*

A lot of people are building up a rivalry between Connors and me. They don't want to see
an everyday match. They want to see someone
dead*

Last year I was trying to do well at Wimbledon. This year I want to win*

Sure he's a great player—but he's also the little
creep tennis reporters and officials could cheerfully throttle   *The People*

If he could accept that everyone makes mistakes—even him—it would help   *Daily Telegraph*

I missed a ball and they clapped. They do it
just to get a reaction from me*

I'm no angel. I never will be*

I can't tell you I'm a nice guy and expect you
to believe it*

That kid will be back. You get a lot of shooting stars who burn themselves out but not McEnroe. He's got too much class for that   *Erik van
Dillen*

I make a hell of a lot more money than I deserve to be making for hitting a tennis ball
across a net*

* John McEnroe

The McEnroe mystique was compounded over the next
few years. People wanted to know what he thought, what he
ate, why he played so well, what his goals were and why he
was so surly. McEnroe was not branded a trouble-maker at
first but was more charitably described as complex and
serious. He didn't stay in the limelight after Wimbledon but
went instead to study economics at Stanford University in
California. He packed his bags and went to school in order to

get the solid grounding in a profession that would save him from coaching rich kids in some resort or summer camp when his championship days were over.

At Stanford he is remembered, not altogether surprisingly, as a gifted natural. His table manners as much as his tennis are now legendary. Chairman of the English department, Robert Polhemus says they were appalling. 'He never shut his mouth until the food dripped out.' Friends of McEnroe said they could spot the place in the canteen where he'd been eating because of the residual debris. He is reported to have enjoyed campus life and to have been a good student despite outside tennis commitments. Churlish with journalists and uncomfortable with the star status that being at Stanford inevitably produced, his public behaviour sometimes bordered on the shifty. He is also remembered at Stanford for playing excellent ping-pong with a frying pan.

'He was a pain to deal with. You could address him and never get a response. It was very uncomfortable,' one publicist said. A teacher remembers Mac had trouble with eye contact. 'When he talked to you he scratched his head, his chest and his legs rather than look at you. He was a very highly strung, tense person.'

Others, those among a small and clannish group of old friends and contemporaries, describe him as modest, generous, loyal and fun. Even his enemies will admit that whatever else he is McEnroe is true to himself.

At Stanford McEnroe kept up with 'professional' (McEnroe was still an amateur), tennis as far as was feasible, but concentrated on boosting the success of the college team. Stanford won the intercollegiate title when McEnroe was on their side. He has since appeared in an exhibition match for them, helping to raise $100,000 for their sports programme. When John left university after a year Kay McEnroe said, 'I wish he could have had a normal education but in my heart I knew he was too talented to wait.'

He hadn't exactly neglected the international game. During late 1977, and in the first part of 1978 his tournaments included the US Pro Indoors championships in Philadelphia, when he went down in the semis to Brian Gottfried, the Volvo Classic in Washington where he reached the quarter finals, the Alan King Classic in Las Vegas where he lost to John Newcombe in the second round and the Rawlings International tournament in London where he lost 8-6, 9-7 to Tony Roche in the final. All was leading, of course, to Wimbledon 1978.

In the Rawlings final at Queens both men were left-handers. The match was the culmination of the warmly anticipated return of Mac to Britain and his progress was monitored closely. To reach the final he'd first beaten his lofty six foot five-inch doubles partner, Peter Fleming, then El Shafei of Egypt, next Gene Mayer of America, dropping a set only to Fleming. Both his quarter final match with Tom Gullikson and his semi with Dibley had gone to three sets and the final itself was a tense double tie breaker despite the straight sets scoreline. The thirty-three-year-old unseeded Roche had to work hard for his win as by now McEnroe was ranked fifteenth in the world and seeded No. 11 at Wimbledon.

Trained on clay and preferring—he usually says—to play on acrylic-painted concrete, the grass of Wimbledon really isn't McEnroe's favourite surface. But he was in fine form, shooting to kill and apparently in good spirits when the championships opened. Having turned professional only weeks earlier, the novelty of playing for money was still with him. After his quarter final win at Queens he'd said, 'This is my first tournament pay day. It's a nice feeling.' The holder of the intercollegiate singles title still had a major pro crown to win and spoke of his career in tennis with a disarming cheeriness which it is hard to imagine these days. 'I keep working away at the basics of my game, aiming at consistency. Okay, I know that if I get lucky I can have a good result against anybody. What I want to do now is play the same high-level game day in and day out.'

It must have been a seethingly disappointed McEnroe who, days later, was eliminated from Wimbledon in his opening match. He lost 7-5, 1-6, 8-9, 6-4, 6-3, to fellow American Erik van Dillen. As can be deduced from the scoreline, it was a long and fiercely fought match with the McEnroe serve and slicing volleys dominating the second and third sets and a display of his cool nerve in the tie break.

It all made for three hours of absorbing tennis. Inexperience may have been at the root of McEnroe's failure, and his pay for that day's work was a princely $394. He did rather better in the doubles where he and Fleming reached the semi-final and picked up $2805 apiece. They went out to the veteran pair Bob Hewitt and Frew McMillan. After the van Dillen match McEnroe appeared to be close to tears. He left the court with a towel over his head. The unseeded van Dillen was generous. 'That kid will be back. You get a lot of shooting stars who burn themselves out but not McEnroe. He's got too much class for that.'

McEnroe, clearly furious with himself for the first round disaster just as he had seemed to be running into blazing form, was petulant with photographers afterwards. At 4-3 up in the fourth set he had seemed assured of taking the match, but he'd blown it. 'You just don't expect to find guys playing out of their skins in the first round of Wimbledon,' he said. 'Yes, I'm taking it pretty hard. I expect more of myself.'

Mac's apparently flagging form was shown to be on the rise again when shortly afterwards, back in the U.S.A. he reached the semis of the Forest Hills Invitational before going out to Nastase in straight sets, although there was a 7-6 tie-break set before he succumbed. This time the pocket money was much more substantial. He banked a cheque for $25,000 and was well on the way towards his current millionaire status. More tournaments in Washington and New Jersey, followed by the US Open Clay Court championships at Indianapolis added such experience and momentum that McEnroe's ratings were zooming with almost every match. By January 1979 he would be ranked fifth in the world.

On clay in Indianapolis, McEnroe met Connors in the quarter finals. After a flying start and the capture of the first set 6-3, he collapsed, and the second and third went to Connors 6-1, 6-1. Days later he was playing in the Canadian Open, reaching the last eight but going down ignominiously 6-1, 6-2, to Eddie Dibbs. In the quarter finals of another tournament on the U.S. circuit, the Pro Championships in Boston, he lost again, 6-2, 6-2, to Harold Solomon. In between the major championships which are widely reported,

Service without a smile.

(Photo: Eamonn McCabe/The Observer)

the group of professional tennis players on the circuit can play every week of the year in some town or resort. Almost every state capital in America has its event and there are others, similar, all over the world. By success or failure at such matches the players' world ratings are decided and ratings can be important when it comes to advertising endorsements and so forth. It's hardly a terrible life to be paid handsomely to do the thing you enjoy but for hard-working members of the professional group, like McEnroe, it is no life of ease either. Of course regular play in smaller tournaments is essential in gaining experience in playing other people on the circuit, but often such matches pall when compared to the major, charismatic championships.

In September 1978 came one such event, the US Open at Flushing Meadow, the championships that McEnroe was preparing for in the anti climactic weeks since Wimbledon. He defeated Sherwood Stewart, Fillol, Peter Fleming, Dowdeswell and Butch Walts to meet Connors in the semi-final. Once again Jimmy proved that he was still very much the top American dog and was very anxious to remain so. He dispensed rapidly with McEnroe in the first two sets, 6-2, 6-2. Although Mac fought back and there was a tie break at the end of the third, the set finished at 7-5.

The tournaments went on and the victories finally began to come. He beat South African Johan Kriek in the United Technologies Classic in Connecticut, then Stockton in the TransAmerica Open in San Francisco. In the final of the Swiss indoor championships he lost to Vilas, but by now the appearance of McEnroe in the last two, four or eight of any event was no longer any sort of surprise. The bank balance was climbing as steadily as the place in the ratings. Another $3,315 after losing to Fibak in the semi-finals of the Cologne Cup in West Germany, and then it was time for perhaps his most interesting match of the year.

In November 1978 Borg and McEnroe met on court. It was not for the first time. Five years earlier, during the US Open they'd met on the clay and had probably exchanged a few words. Borg was competing, as tennis's sensational blonde *wunderkind* and McEnroe was a ball boy. It's probably on film somewhere. Mac must have done OK. They asked him to return as a ball boy the next year.

However, the first time they met as duellists, with the ritual twenty-six paces between them and rackets as their chosen weaponry, was in the semi-final of the Swedish Open in Stockholm, Borg's home turf. McEnroe had not dropped a set in any of the preceding four matches and he beat Borg in straight sets. Easily: 6-3, 6-4. It is astonishing that so little was made of this match, Borg's first ever defeat to a younger player. Perhaps back in 1978 McEnroe was not yet seriously seen as tennis's heir apparent. He won the final, too. 6-2, 6-2, against Tim Gullikson.

When he flew to England a few days later it was to play in the Benson and Hedges Tournament at Wembley, an event which has since then become closely linked with McEnroe. Firstly he demolished David Lloyd, brother of John Lloyd, 6-4, 6-2. Then he set about Tom Okker and went to a 6-2, 6-4 win. Next he beat Barazzutti in the quarter finals, 6-0, 7-6. In the semi finals he took only seventy minutes to polish off fellow-American Dick Stockton after a slow start, 6-4, 6-3. Great volleying and net play gave him a hard time in the first set, coupled with a little difficulty with his serve. Stockton broke serve once in the second set, but McEnroe immediately broke back and the set was over in less than half an hour.

The final, with Tim Gullikson, was more of a match, going to four sets and two tie-breaks. As in many of these circuit tournaments, preliminary matches can be decided on a best of three sets basis, but the final has to be the best of five, in the classic fashion. Hatchet-faced and tight-muscled, McEnroe faced this match with the now familiar grim intensity. Gullikson, too, was taking it very seriously indeed. For him it was a chance to heave himself upwards into the very front rank of tennis internationals. For McEnroe victory would almost certainly represent a ticket to the Colgate Masters tournament in New York in January. In the points system devised by the organisers of the international tennis circuit, a victory in one tournament or an accumulation of good performances will earn a player the right to play at some of the more exclusive or invitational tournaments. Thus it is not only the prestige of the moment or the prize money that is at stake.

Some events are deemed less important than others and players will sometimes opt out voluntarily—few of them want to play fifty-two weeks a year. But the Colgate Masters is regarded by the world's professionals as one of the key events on the tennis calendar and competition to take part in it is heated. It is, perhaps, one of the events which lends the 'playboy circus' image of the elite group of players who zip round the world for tennis tournaments a kind of seriousness which is sometimes fudged amidst talk of prize money and 'minor' matches in towns that no-one has ever heard of.

The match with Gullikson was a repeat of the previous week's Stockholm final in some ways, but played with more vehemence. McEnroe had set point at 5-4, but Gullikson took the game and then there was spatting during the tie-break when it stood at 6-5 to Gullikson. After three minutes arguing a point which had been awarded to Gullikson, the umpire gave in to McEnroe and reversed the decision. Gullikson took the tie break all the same, and thus the first set, 7-6. McEnroe took the second, 6-4, and Gullikson was looking weary. He rallied, however, and McEnroe had to work hard all the way through to another tie-break to take the set 7-6. Despite both men's exhaustion the final set was a grittily fought one, too, belying the score of 6-2. When it was all over both men looked spent.

It was McEnroe's first major triumph in Britain and his anger at times during the match compounded his fast-growing 'Superbrat' image here, for the foreseeable future. Accused of stalling, glaring and intimidating tactics to get the tie-break point decision reversed, he was an unpopular champion. He won £18,200 that night, and a great many more enemies.

The next major event on his schedule was the final of the Davis Cup in which Great Britain were meeting the USA Due to take place in December in Palm Springs, it was heart-warming for Britains to find that the home team had made it to the final. Now ranked sixth in the world, McEnroe was an important member of the American side and despite saying that he didn't regard the Davis Cup as anything exceptional

—not exactly the kind of remark likely to endear him to British tennis watchers—he showed no signs of treating tennis less seriously when playing for his country than when he plays for John McEnroe and the money.

He did more than anyone else to bring the Davis Cup back to the States for the first time since 1972, conceding only ten games in two matches. Starting with two aces in his match with John Lloyd he then floored Buster Mottram. In the Lloyd match he took only an hour and forty minutes to reach a decisive 6-1, 6-2, 6-2 score. It wasn't really fair on Lloyd who did well to get to get to deuce once or twice. McEnroe was in such stunning form he looked as if he could have saved time and played Mottram simultaneously.

When Buster's turn came he was blasted 6-2, 6-2, 6-1, and the Davis Cup was back in America for the twenty-fifth time in fifty years. Mottram had briefly ignited British hopes when he beat Brian Gottfried on the opening day, but the hard court, McEnroe's speed, wondrous angled shots and the blistering heat of Palm Springs stymied Mottram's chances. Shouting 'Too fast, too fast' at one especially dizzy series of passes from McEnroe, Mottram played close to the base line for much of the game. Mac said afterwards that he didn't think this had been 'particularly smart'.

Around now several aspects of McEnroe's sporting and personal personality were being solidified. Tales were told out of school, like the one about McEnroe's argy bargy with a stylishly turned-out blonde who applauded a double fault during a match in California.

'Doncha know you're not supposed to do that?' he raged, hands typically placed on his hips. Minutes later in the same match he had what he considered to be a bad line call from a judge wearing sunglasses. McEnroe enquired why he was wearing shades when there was no sun, positing the possibility that the man was, in fact, blind. Since then McEnroe has held forth about elderly umpires—they shouldn't be allowed to adjudicate on account of their advanced years and, presumably, approaching senility. At the times such remarks were held to be the height of bad manners but the worst was to come.

McEnroe, like all the professionals on the grand prix

circuit, has to play three small non-grand prix tournaments a year to qualify for entry to main events. In 1978 he'd chosen to play one of these in San José, close to his old campus at Stanford and he approached the little contest with as much ferocity as for any major event. The small tournament got full houses every night he played. A certain amount of racket bashing (or, as it is quaintly termed in the official code of conduct, racket abuse), took place, some sharp retorts to photographers and an irritated kick here and there injected the usual level of rowdiness. Yet he seemed genuinely dismayed afterwards when asked about it all. 'Look, there were definitely some bad calls out there tonight in my opinion and there wasn't a lot I could do about it. I don't care if they make mistakes. I expect them to make mistakes. I just want them to admit to them.'

McEnroe is quite ready to concede a point which he feels has been wrongly awarded to him by a bad call, but the fact that this happens quite often is seldom mentioned when there is uproar over his own attempts to argue about points which he feels should be his. Similarly much was made, at Wimbledon 1981, of his enquiry to the umpire during a match with Amritraj if 'Indian' umpiring was going on. A most tactless and unfortunate way to register dismay and one which earned him accusations of racialism. McEnroe is reported to have turned down a flat $1,000,000 rather than play in an exhibition tournament in South Africa, so he needs little defending against such charges. Connors joined McEnroe in the charity match for the World Hunger Project which took place at the same time. It is arguable that McEnroe's decision to play for a good cause was based on cynical 'image improvement' motives, or even for tax reasons, but I think this is unlikely.

At the Colgate Masters tournament at the turn of 1978, McEnroe was one of six Americans in the final eight. Madison Square Gardens in New York is a traditional venue for spectacular boxing matches and is also noted for the restlessness of the crowds there. If McEnroe dislikes the shuffling and milling around the rather shabby Wimbledon court two, the heckling, rush-hour atmosphere of Madison Square Gardens must be even more unsettling. The crowd are not seat-bound and reverent: rather they move about, chatter, flip the tops of beer cans and stuff their faces with hot-dogs with little regard for either fellow-spectators or for the competitors. Since Borg was not taking part in this year's event, the Masters was seen as a testing ground for the two great American heavy-weights and expectations were that Connors and McEnroe would go the full distance in the final.

In an early (but not eliminating), round McEnroe spent only fifty-five minutes in dispatching Arthur Ashe 6-3, 6-1 and Connors made similarly short work of Harold Solomon. Connors was the crowd's favourite, winning his early matches to ringing cheers of 'Go Jimmy', whilst McEnroe's early matches were watched with a more detatched interest. Connors was the title holder and Mac had yet to beat him. At that stage of his career his rivalry with Jimmy was stronger than that with Borg. McEnroe was fighting for recognition as the world's No. 2 player, but in four meetings with Connors, notably in the 1977 Wimbledon semi finals and the US Open semi of 1978, he had yet to break through.

Like the best prize fights—the prize here being roughly £50,000—the defender and the contender were goaded into pre-match predictions. Such engineered needle has never been neccessary with these two men as neither has ever had any trouble in speaking their mind nor is there any particular personal friendship between them. Dressed in a camel-hair overcoat as befits a boxing venue McEnroe stated before their match that he was looking forward to it, had high hopes of a win and was happy with his form. He was well aware of the challenge Connors represented. 'I always feel I'm being rushed when I play him,' he said.

Jimbo for his part was also in fighting spirits. After his match with Solomon he said he felt so good he hadn't wanted the game to end. 'I'm just happy to be playing in the Garden. Any time I can play in a place where Ali has fought that's good enough for me.' He went on to eulogise about New York and New Yorkers to the point where one elderly city resident muttered something about the main attraction of playing in the Big Apple being somehow related to big cheques. And he wasn't talking about Ivan Lendl.

After all that it was a technical knock-out. When

McEnroe was a set up, 7-5 after a tie-break, and leading 3-0 in the second Connors withdrew with a foot injury. If he'd played just another three games and allowed the set to go to McEnroe he could have withdrawn at the break and given himself the option of continuing the match the following day. But mysteriously he simply gave up. Afterwards McEnroe had mixed feelings. He was pleased, he said, to have beaten Connors, any way of winning against Jimmy was better than no way at all, but he'd have preferred to have won by fighting it through.

So it was, after all, Arthur Ashe (who'd had successes in his later rounds), that McEnroe met in the final of the Colgate Masters and he beat him in straight sets, 6-7, 6-3, 7-5. It was a good week for Mac, as he and Fleming also won the doubles, beating Okker and Fibak 6-4, 6-2, 6-4.

Things went on rosily. In January 1979 he and Fleming won the Braniff Airways world doubles championships at Olympia in London, beating Bob Hewitt and Frew McMillan of South Africa 6-3, 6-3, although McEnroe had suffered a heavy fall at the start of the second set. McMillan raised his famous white cap to McEnroe. 'It was devastating', he said. The two couples had met in the previous Wimbledon final where the old stagers had beaten the new boys. McEnroe was moving into ominously sharp form.

The tournaments and triumphs continued into 1979. In March he beat Connors again in straight sets in the US indoor championships (7-6, 7-6), having crushed South African Bernie Mitton to reach the final and later that month he met Borg again in the semi final of the New Orleans Tennis Festival. In an atmosphere that must have been anything but Mardi Gras, he took the match 5-7, 6-1, 7-6. Borg summed things up afterwards. 'Last time we met, in Richmond Virginia earlier this year I was lucky because John had eight match points, and I won. Maybe this time he was lucky because I had two match points and lost. Both times the result could have been different.'

This match however, was a cut and thrust above the Richmond clash. Borg at twenty-two and Mac at twenty were two young men at the very peak of physical strength and the notion of seeing any confrontation between them as a duel between devastating equals was now established. The New Orleans game was graced by artistry and brilliance. There were breath-taking spinning lobs and flicking passing shots. There were also rare moments of good humour. At one point McEnroe lay prone for several seconds, having hurled himself headlong to meet one of Borg's backhands. Bjorn lay down in sympathy until McEnroe had recovered.

With the first set going to Borg, the second to Mac and the third culminating in a taut tie break, it had all the makings of a small classic. The tie break finished with a marvellous cross court volley from McEnroe which even Borg could not reach. By seven points to five McEnroe took the break, the set and the match.

They met again the following month at the ABN Bank tournament in Rotterdam. Borg, who'd obliterated Peter Fleming 6-2, 6-2 in the semi-final levelled the score to two all this time. It was his first appearance in the final of this event in four tries. Two poor backhand volleys in the first game of the match gave McEnroe a bad start. 'I never really recovered from those stupid mistakes.' They lost him his service and thereafter it was an uphill struggle to keep level, let alone get ahead. There were some powerful rallies and Mac threw himself around the court with his usual rattlesnake speed, but Borg's service was invincible that day and McEnroe never once managed to hold break point. Borg won 6-4, 6-2.

Shortly before the Rotterdam final McEnroe had caused a few British hearts to flutter when he was drawn against the unfancied Andrew Jarrett, ranked 127th in the world and playing in his first 32-man pro tournament. Jarrett took the first set valiantly, 6-4. But McEnroe's reply was a cursory 6-1, 6-2 dismissal in the two last sets. 'It was like trying to stop a river', said Jarrett afterwards of the McEnroe serve. Mac had pounded fourteen aces at him. As many of McEnroe's victims have said, Jarrett reported that his downfall came with that punishing left-hand serve that can make the ball swing any way Mac chooses. McEnroe went on to meet and similarly dismiss Buster Mottram in their battle for a place in the quarter finals of the tournament.

In May 1979 McEnroe took the WCT crown in Dallas, routing Jimmy Connors in the semis and Borg again in the final, 7-5, 4-6, 6-2, 7-6. So the circus rolled on towards Wimbledon 1979. Just before arriving in Britain, the new menace of tennis met the old master of disaster. Nasty and Superbrat played against each other in Jamaica and between them they reduced an elderly woman line judge to tears. At times the umpire, twitching in his high chair, seemed to have lost control of the match. When a ball from McEnroe caught Nastase on the back of his neck the crowd expected some kind of volcanic erruption, but Nastase simply remarked coolly that 'He is worse than me and Connors put together.'

'I die. Sometimes I just die,' said his mother.

'Look, I don't go out of my way to have the crowd against me. It can be a big handicap, but hell, you have to stand up for your rights,' said John McEnroe.

He arrived in England to play in the pre-Wimbledon Stella Artois tournament at Queens. After a quiet start and appearing to be keeping his promise about being a good boy, he hit big trouble in his third round match with Vijay Amitraj of India. Right from the pre-match knockabout he seemed to be in contentious form. He told umpire Dick Lumb that he wanted more time to warm up but after five more practice serves he still wasn't ready. Squadron Leader Lumb announced that play must begin. Since it didn't, he awarded a penalty point and subsequently a game against McEnroe. There was now a ten minute delay while McEnroe raged. McEnroe's ire may well have been well justified but he over-reacted, just a bit. 'He's won the match if he's won the game', he declared. Tournament director Clive Bernstein, referee Jim Moore and grand prix supervisor Frank Smith were all called over. 'I was waiting to play the second point. It makes me sick. I want him off the chair.' McEnroe was furious. Meanwhile Amritraj was taking a leaf out of Connors' *How to be a Good Actor* book, had changed ends and was playing his second game with an invisible opponent, rather like the famous scene in *Blow Up*. The officials at last decided that a technical officiating error had been made and declared the match to stand at love-all.

McEnroe had not succeeded in unchairing the umpire and his concentration suffered badly for the next few games. It was during this period that the oft-quoted and outraged

(A) Arguing the point. Wimbledon, 1979.
(Daily Telegraph Colour Library)

(B) McEnroe mobbed by fans.
(Photo: Paul Harris/Daily Telegraph Colour Library)

enquiry 'Are you in the human race?' was made to a hapless woman spectator. There was another exchange with the umpire but eventually McEnroe settled down and took the set 7-6 and won the match by dismissing Amitraj 6-1 in the second set. After the match McEnroe said all he'd wanted was another few seconds to get ready and the uproar that had ensued when the umpire had commanded that play should begin was both unneccessary and, for him, damagingly distracting.

'Some tennis was taken away because of what happened,' said McEnroe. This is in answer to the commonly held view that the crowds come to see a game, not a fight. Mac agrees: he'd rather play tennis than argue, but he's unable to bear officialdom which he sees as downright wrong. He also said something after that match which may do more to explain some of his attitudes toward crowds than almost anything else. I know he's a big, rich boy now, but there's something cogent and touching about this: 'I said a few things to the crowd. That's my fault to respond, but when they clap your double faults and call you ugly . . .'

McEnroe stated later that he knew his anti-authoritarian stance cost him dearly, but it doesn't seem to make much difference. Ultimately he's willing to risk the loss of penalty points, fines or even disqualification in his insistence on what he feels is fair. These sort of risks are as much part of his attitude to the game as the risks he takes in his tennis. There's no sign that his tactics will help him to get the fair treatment he sometimes feels he is denied, or that he will give up his artlessly undiplomatic and tactless methods.

The next uproar came in a blistering exchange with a familiar foe, Sandy Mayer. In the sixth game, after a disputed service call in his quarter-final match McEnroe demanded to know the umpire's name and vowed that he'd never go on court with him again. The umpire, Roy Cope-Lewis calmly gave Mac his moniker and a penalty point. Enter Jim Moore and Frank Smith again. This time the penalty stuck. Scowling throughout the rest of the match McEnroe nonetheless dispensed with Mayer who said afterwards that McEnroe is punished less than he deserves. He advocated disqualification for five or six matches. There is little love lost between these two men. Next came the semi-final match with Roscoe Tanner. It was a morose and subdued Mac who took the match 6-4, 7-5. 'I don't think I'm a hundred percent right, there's no doubt about that. But the umpires are now, I think, a little quick on me,' he said later.

In the final against pin-up boy Victor Pecci of Paraguay he behaved like a young conservative, except there was no braying or hooraying. It was a model performance and near effortless, 6-7, 6-1, 6-1, win. A tough start but a clinical finish and nairy a tremor of discontent. If he was tense at all it showed only in the number of times he double-faulted: five times in the eighth game of the match. He won that game eventually, and double faulting has always been a barometer of the kind of chances McEnroe is prepared to take in his game. He was razor sharp in the last two sets, never double faulted again and took home a cheque for £9,392.

At Wimbledon he was seeded No. 2. There was a classic upset, the kind that happens almost every year and the one which that year, one guesses, was the surprise that some might have prayed to St. Dan, the patron saint of tennis for. After a fairly easy passage to the third round McEnroe was devastated by a spirited performance by Tim Gullikson. His thigh was bandaged heavily, he didn't feel or look well and we went out 6-4, 6-2, 6-4. A dazed and dismayed McEnroe said afterwards that the rain, the miserable cold and the old ankle injury had contributed to his defeat, but he was generous about Gullikson. 'He was a better man on the day.' McEnroe had a cold, he felt sore, his leg hurt but I don't think he was making excuses—merely seeking explanations.

When the No. 2 seed is knocked out by an underdog the public response is usually pretty vivid. In McEnroe's case it was surprisingly mixed. Whilst some pundits clearly rejoiced in his come-uppance others took a more sympathetic view. One noted that it had been unfair on McEnroe to have to play twice on the notoriously difficult and uneven surface of court two. Some said that army captain umpire Ron Crickmore had been less than well-mannered in addressing him as 'McEn-roe' whilst he called instructions to 'Mr. Gullikson.' That kind of thing could have unsettled McEnroe, as could the unusually loud audience participation which had gone unadmonished. Yes, some sympathy for the loser.

Potato face had had his chips. Wimbledon had given him the tennis elbow. Tearful teenaged girls also proved that some people, at least, were sorry to see him knocked out of Wimbledon again. There had been some lovely rallies in the match, even on that cramped outside court. The limping McEnroe had managed to pull round a bit in the third set, raising some hopes and cheers, and in his defeat he may even have gained a few more sympathisers. But it was, on the whole, a popular defeat and it began to be wondered if the McEnroe machine was all mouth after all.

Where Wimbledon was concerned, certainly, he didn't seem to have it in him to fulfil his promise or display the form that other, lesser tournaments coaxed out of him. McEnroe had called a line judge a nit picker for foot-faulting him. 'I never foot fault.' Gullikson had been able to capitalise on the fact that, for once, McEnroe's serve was letting him down. At one point, from two all in the second set, McEnroe lost eight games in a row. Not even McEnroe could recover from being two sets down that day, especially when he was 4-0 down in the third. As the scoreline shows he rallied and saved a match point at 5-4. By McEnroe's standards it was a slow and lifeless game although fifteenth seeded Gullikson's attack made it interesting.

'I felt awful at the start. These muscle strains always come at the wrong time, but I'm not going to stay in bed for two months before Wimbledon just to make sure I don't get hurt. I guess Bjorn has a good chance now—he wins it every other year and I'm sure that's what the British crowds want.' McEnroe's remarks were tinged with bitterness. Borg did, of course win, against Roscoe Tanner in the final. There was some compensation for McEnroe as he and Fleming took the doubles title, but shortly afterwards there was more disappointment for Mac when he lost the Canadian Open to Borg. The summer of 1979 was pretty miserable.

Two months later there was massive consolation. It may, in fact, only be British chauvinism that consigns the US Open—or any other tournament—a notch or two beneath Wimbledon. For McEnroe his triumph at Flushing Meadow was a moment to be savoured. 'This is the best feeling about tennis I've ever had. If I never win it again I'll be happy with once.'

On the hard surface he favours and just ten minutes drive away from the family home, McEnroe at last won one of the world's four most important titles. The Masters, the WCT, the Braniff Doubles and the other professional circuit high spots, after all, represent victory over as few as seven other competitors. Like Wimbledon and the other points on the grand slam compass, Paris and Melbourne, at Flushing Meadow the final pair have been weeded out of an original 128 players.

McEnroe met Nastase during an early round and during this joyless match had a few sharp words for the inevitable woman who clapped the inevitable double fault. 'Good serve, wasn't it lady? Wasn't that a nice double fault? Did you like it? You're sick, lady. You should stay home.'

A combination of the jets shrieking away from La Guardia, just a few miles away, the television cameras and hostile audiences made things look, early on, as if McEnroe's concentration was damaged and the strains of the summer still sore. But McEnroe overcame the distractions and breezed through the tournament, dismissing Connors in straight sets in the semi-finals.

If he was looking forward to a chance to take on Borg in the final, he was to be disappointed as, stymied here as usual, Borg fell to Roscoe Tanner in the quarter finals. Still chasing a U.S. Open win Borg was said to be so disenchanted with the organisation of the Flushing Meadow event that if he had won he would not have bothered to return to defend the title the following year. However, until he captures this title we can probably expect him to compete there. He's superstitious —never shaves during Wimbledon and that might have helped him psychologically during his long run of wins there. So maybe it would help if he had a little ritual for Flushing Meadow. A hair cut, or a false nose perhaps . . .

So McEnroe faced fellow-New Yorker, Vitas Gerulaitis in the final. 'I was so nervous it was a joke,' he said later. Vitas's natty yellow outfit could not assist him in the bombardment from McEnroe, who suddenly found all the roaring form that had eluded him all summer. In straight sets —7-5, 6-3, 6-3—he astonished the capacity crowd in the great concrete bowl with the extent to which his talent had matured since last year. He only had to struggle once during the match—in the first set when he lost his serve at 5-4 for the only time in the match. After winning the tie-break his serve and volley attack served as an invincible foundation for a marvellously plotted assault in which he seemed to have devised his moves—and Vitas's—three shots in advance.

He won on his first match point, flung his racket into the air and leapt in jubilation. This caused the one sour incident of the match, since the spectator who caught it wanted to keep it, rather as the hopeful bridesmaids scrabble to catch the bridal bouquet. But the guards insisted on returning it to McEnroe and the spectator was thus robbed of a superstitious chance to become the next Flushing bride. After his win McEnroe was awarded a special citation from New York mayor, Ed Koch, for having brought the trophy back to the city.

It was the year of the brats at Flushing Meadow. Young Tracy Austin beat Chris Evert that year in the ladies singles. At sixteen, she was the youngest-ever winner.

Neither Borg nor McEnroe competed in the fourth stage of the grand slam, in Melbourne, each preferring to spend Christmas at home since neither had a chance of achieving the slam. With McEnroe's win in the States and Borg's at Wimbledon and Paris, the spoils were already divided. Mac said he might have gone to Australia to offer 'token resistance' if Borg had elected to play.

In November 1979 McEnroe flew back to London—his eighth visit—to play in the Benson and Hedges Tournament at Wembley. It was calculated that for each of the ninety days or so that he had spent in England up to then his earnings had averaged about £700. But money isn't everything and he had strong words to say about England, immediately telling journalists that he was not to be expected back in January to defend his Braniff doubles crown. Of training facilities for youngsters in Britain he was withering. 'You don't give them anything. No chance, no help. The Vanderbilt Club (closely associated with the Benson and Hedges event), is supposed to be the best indoor club but its 20 degrees below freezing there and Queens is just as terrible.' Some of his most savage indictments were reserved for the holy of holies. Speaking of the previous summer at Wimbledon he said he hadn't enjoyed anything about it and he even advocated some changes for the sacred turf.

Grass, he said, was out-dated. 'It's ridiculous that the most important event of the year should be played on grass.' He recommended that the lawns be ploughed up and replaced with a hard surface. To what extent these remarks were pure mischief, or some kind of dour and mindless revenge can only be guessed but ironically his comments about training facilities for young players could not have come at a better time for Paul Hutchins, Britain's Davis Cup coach who was campaigning for a Port Washington style centre.

After his words about Wimbledon the secretary of the All England Club, Chris Golling remarked drily that he wondered what McEnroe would say about grass when he won Wimbledon. Interesting—his comments implied that a McEnroe win there eventually was a foregone conclusion. And to reassure those who might fear that there was the barest chance that McEnroe's advice would be followed, he added, 'Rest assured Wimbledon will keep its grass for the forseeable future, though the number two court will be made safer for the next championship.'

McEnroe was unstoppable and pugnacious throughout the Benson and Hedges week, his nineteenth grand prix event of the year. He made short work of John Lloyd, the nearest thing Britain has to a blonde bombshell. 'You can't pick out what he's going to do. He cuts it, spins it and it's devastating,' said Lloyd afterwards. Next he took less than an hour to dispense with Britain's No. 4, the old Etonian Robin Drysdale. The score was 6-2, 6-2. Drysdale had played McEnroe once before, in Washington, and had put up a creditable performance to go down 7-5, 6-2, but in their Wembley match, despite McEnroe's erratic serving (he had six double faults to match his six aces), McEnroe was on very bankable form. In the quarter finals he met Wojtek Fibak of Poland and took the match 6-2, 6-1. The scoreline is deceptive. The fifth game of the 52 minute opening set went to 22 points and nine deuces and Fibak eventually broke through McEnroe's serve.

The furore towards the end of this game typifies the kind of trouble McEnroe gets into and the reasons why he often feels himself ill-served by officials. After the ninth deuce McEnroe lobbed a shot which was perilously close to the line but was, in fact, just in. At any rate the linesman thought so and called the ball good. However a shout of 'Out' from a spectator led Fibak to think the ball was bad, so he casually flipped the ball over the net for McEnroe to serve again. McEnroe did not play the ball and the umpire called for the point to be replayed. McEnroe took violent issue with this and only after a four minute wrangle with the referee and the grand prix supervisor did he reluctantly agree to play on. Two points later he double faulted and the game was Fibak's. However, he lost only one more game in his progress to the semi-finals and left the court to grudging applause mingled with slow hand-claps.

He went on to beat Gianni Ocleppo in the semi and finally won the championship with a somewhat lacklustre win over Harold Solomon the following Sunday.

In the final of the US indoor championships at Philadelphia, McEnroe went down to Connors in five sets: 6-3, 2-6, 6-3, 3-6, 6-4. In three and a quarter hours of blistering, grunting aggression, no quarter was asked or given. The tempo of these matches between Connors and McEnroe was by now familiar. Tired, possibly, from a heavy programme the day before, during which he'd had a four set semi against John Sadri and three tie breaking sets with Fleming to win the doubles, McEnroe was a shade below peak form. Gambling, as so often, on his second service, he double faulted consistently in the Connors match. However, the fifth set was a real heart-stopper. A service break down on three occasions he pulled round twice but could not manage the vital third recovery.

The previous day Connors had needed less than an hour and a half to beat Gene Mayer whose remarks after the game, along with those of his brother Sandy, assumed a familiar note of bruised complaint. Speaking of Connors' groin injury he said, 'Other people play down their injuries. Jimmy plays them up. We won easily against Ramirez and then Fibak. I wish my groin hurt like that!'

The Connors McEnroe final gave the crowd every cent of their money's worth and Connors was a deserving victor. In retrospect the match can be seen to mark the beginning of a long—though not entirely uninterrupted—loss of form that led McEnroe to face Wimbledon in 1980 with a recent history of many defeats and a grudge nestling firmly amongst the other chips on his shoulder.

While there were some high points early in 1980, notably the victory over Amitraj in the final of one leg of the WCT grand prix in Milan that March, McEnroe was not exactly blazing. In the points system he led the pro rankings, but he was finding the big, spectacular, prestigious wins hard to find. He was beaten again by Connors in the WCT match in Dallas and by Gerulaitis at Forest Hills in May. Going down 2-6, 6-2, 0-6 before a home crowd, it was his eleventh defeat of the year and the third successive time that Vitas had bested him. This match, played in biting winds and rain (which blew and fell, of course, on Gerulaitis too, but McEnroe has always been unusually affected by nasty weather conditions) was umpired by Fred Hoyles who would have been unlikely to allow play to continue in such conditions at Wimbledon.

Despite protestations from Mac the match went ahead. Perhaps the television sponsorship which underwrote expenses had something to do with this. While Gerulaitis took it all in his enormous stride, McEnroe's game was affected by heavy balls and a slithery surface. He was less aggressive than usual, both technically and verbally. People wondered whether the rest he had taken recently had hindered rather than helped his game. The edge was absent. Despite fine rallies, his service was shakey and he admitted afterwards that he'd been playing too much and needed another rest before Wimbledon.

As Connors seemed rejuvenated and McEnroe's run of defeats continued into the summer people started to talk about the rise and fall of Superbrat, began to see Connors, once again, as Borg's main rival and to wonder if the McEnroe challenge was too fragile to resist the pressures of the pro circuit. His thigh and ankle injuries hung around. In many pictures he looked dejected to the point of desolation. Players like Harold Solomon and Jose Luis Clerc of Argentina were whisking matches away where in 1979 they would have been pushed to take a set. McEnroe was almost beginning to be written off.

(A) Superdad. McEnroe Snr. applauds his son during the US Open, 1980.
(Allsport Photographic)

) Mac wins the US Open, throwing up his arms in victory over Borg.
(Associated Press)

6

THE STILETTO

Connors is an animal, Borg is a machine, McEnroe is an artist   *David Benjamin, Princetown University coach*

He has so much touch it's ridiculous   *Vitas Gerulaitis*

This guy is a stiletto, he just slices people up   *Arthur Ashe*

One of the most phenomenally gifted young players to ever walk onto a tennis court   *Daily Telegraph*

His serve is the best   *Bjorn Borg*

If someone tries to prise a point away from him they might just as well be trying to take a dying man's last drop of water in the desert   *Henry Raven*

McEnroe hits the ball harder and volleys better than Borg and his serve is more deceptive   *Roscoe Tanner*

Junior has great balance. He's got a ton of shots. It's slice here, nick there, cut over here. Pretty soon you've got blood all over you. He's the best player in the world right *now*   *Arthur Ashe*

Sure I like to win. It's all that really matters to me. I'm a tough competitor and I know it*

Stupid linesman*   [*to himself*]

Nice serve, John*   [*to himself*]

Nobody has ever made me look such an idiot, not even Connors or Borg. I'm not exactly slow around the court but he made me look like an elephant   *John Lloyd*

* *John McEnroe*

Occasionally, amidst the outcries and outrages that punctuate the John McEnroe v Rest of the World mudslinging, the fact that he is a consummate athlete, a master at his game and peerless with certain shots, is almost forgotten. The attention that he draws to himself would not, of course, be so firmly printed on the public consciousness if he was an indifferent player. Whilst it is certain that no ambitious player, however greatly or minimally gifted, is likely to improve their game simply by reading about McEnroe's, it is worth examining some of the facets of his play that have helped him to become the wayward genius of international tennis.

Davis Cup team captain Arthur Ashe said to Bud Collins in the *Observer* in 1979, 'This guy is a stiletto. He just slices people up' and much useful technical description of McEnroe's play is distilled from remarks Ashe made in the American magazine *Tennis* in May 1981.

McEnroe's serve is characterised by his slow upward toss of the ball and his now almost quaintly old-fashioned use of a wooden racket. Despite the fact that McEnroe's shorts have often looked a trifle constricting, despite his laconic, sometimes weary-looking opening throw, that serve is devastating. In many matches, even those he loses, McEnroe will be seen to have served more aces than the other guy. He'll very likely have double faulted more too, because he takes risks with his second serve. McEnroe uses Dunlop rackets and will continue to do so until his contract with the company expires, at least. There is talk of him designing and using his own racket sometime in the future. Although he has tried both graphite and steel rackets they gave him no feel for the ball and he reverted to wood after losing to Mayer and then to Borg in the Masters tournament in New York in 1981.

'He has so much touch it's ridiculous,' Vitas Gerulaitis has said.

'McEnroe doesn't need to bludgeon you because he's enormously talented with the racket. Only a few other guys around handle a racket the way he does. He has very quick hands, he knows just where to put the balls,' said Arthur Ashe.

Former mixed doubles partner Mary Carillo, a few years older than McEnroe and a friend for some years, was a supportive companion during his early tournament years, and has spoken of his perfectionism. 'He has a real sense of beauty about the game. To him everything should be just so. No noise from the fans at the wrong time. Excellent officiating. If something happens that wrecks it for him he gets upset. He believes it's phoney not to show how you feel.'

McEnroe is 5 ft. 11 ins. tall—a fraction taller than a few years ago but still a lot shorter than many of the lanky, long-legged stars on the circuit. Even now, much thinner than when he first played in England and with a leaner silhouette, he still tends to look rather shorter than he really is. As a left-hander he has a built-in advantage over the more common right-hand servers, but his speed on court, range of shots and uncanny accuracy of placement are far greater plusses. He tends to make the other guy look slow. Watching any match after seeing McEnroe dart and dash around a court often emphasises this: the other players will seem to be lumbering a little, whoever they are, until one adjusts to the pace of their game.

McEnroe's instinct and energy are legendary. Even faced with hostility they rarely desert him. In stressed moments he is as likely to win the big point. This often happens in matches with Borg. It is tempting to see these two young men as eternal duellists, perfect foils for contrasting temperaments, almost perfectly matched in skills and virtually guaranteed to make any confrontation a battle royal. Where Borg's composure, backhand and blistering base line passes are usually inviolable, McEnroe's serve, anticipation and volley will even the balance. However, for a number of reasons confrontations between the two giants have been relatively few and are likely to remain rare.

McEnroe has a dislike of exhibition matches. 'You intend to try your hardest, but they are not the same as tournaments because it doesn't matter if you win or lose, and that sort of attitude can harm your competitiveness in the long run,' he said. Borg does not avoid these show-piece games as studiously as McEnroe, but he is carefully managed to play relatively rarely, particularly in Britain. The upshot is that confrontations between these two are usually within major tournaments and thus weighted with an extra drama. It is unlikely that their meetings are actually contrived to be rare, teasing the public into anticipation and expectation, but this is how things have worked out.

In the fairly recent past Laver and Rosewall faced each other hundreds of times over the years but it is unlikely that Borg and McEnroe will meet much more often than half a dozen times a year. Jack Kramer has described the old professional circuit as being something like a tour of roving troupers. Tiring but simple in its repetition. The players got to know one another's games backwards and since sponsorship and prize money was less then than it is today, it was not a particularly glamorous life. These days, with fewer meetings between the giants, travel is more like that of a superstar rock and roller. Since the WCT grand prix circuit was set up in 1971 with events all over the world, it's Concorde and the best hotels, a protective entourage and a choice of venues that can make meetings between any two players quite rare.

The players get to know each other's game almost as much by watching video tapes as by matches. The places where many of the tournaments are held, the prize money and the status that is now bestowed on a top professional makes for an enviable, even pampered lifestyle. It's not a dismal existence, however boring airport lounges or soulless hotel bedrooms can be. But perhaps it is a small miracle that despite a lifestyle of such luxury these men can still produce the sort of biting aggression and determination it takes to win. Luxury usually erodes that neccessary sense of grit and the survival instinct.

The WCT tour culminates in the finals in Dallas. McEnroe won in 1981, having eliminated Borg in the semi-finals in Milan. In that match the McEnroe serve, which he had been honing all winter, had outpaced an uncharacteristically nervy Borg, and McEnroe went on to win both Wimbledon and the US Open. The grand slam was never a possibility as he'd been beaten early in the French Open. Although late in 1981 McEnroe's year closed with a few recent shadows—he was badly dejected by his defeat in the Benson and Hedges tournament in November—it was a period which demonstrated his powers as never before.

Fellow professionals had been praising McEnroe's technique for some years. After the Colgate Masters in 1979, during which he had staved off a number of match points in his match against Ashe in what McEnroe described as the best come-back of his playing career thus far, Ashe said, 'The situation called for a special sort of toughness and he met the challenge. He had to figure it all out for himself—and he did.' Australian John Alexander has said that one of the secrets of McEnroe's success is that he disguises his shots so well.

Every shot in the book seems to be McEnroe's to command. The combination of his serve, speed and the wristy forehand which looks like flick-knife practice and his extraordinary aggression is usually unbeatable. By the time he came to play at the Stella Artois tournament in London in 1981 all these skills—and the sharp tongue—were famous.

Amidst praise, then, for his razor-reflexes and the sort of ESP that enables him to move to precisely the right spot to pick up and return even the most clever shots, there was hand-wringing. He has the ability to return the most savage volleys as if he were flicking away a stray ball back for the other guy's service. The neat flipping movement which can lift a ball over the net never to be returned were all in evidence at the Stella Artois, but so was the temper and it was quite unnecessary since in those matches his form was so superb that success was fairly assured. All of which rather supports the view that the aggression is indeed self-directed abuse: a kind of unfortunate reflex which others sometimes take more seriously than they need to.

Asked shortly afterwards if he, like Borg, wished to be remembered as the best tennis player of all time McEnroe replied that he certainly didn't want to be remembered for *some* of the things he did on court. This was soon after such unfortunate remarks as 'faggot' and 'rubbish' on court. At the same time he spoke of the previous year's final and admitted that Borg had been faster on grass than he had expected him to be and added that it would be boring for the other players on the circuit if Borg went on winning year after year. For a moment it sounded as if he was expressing the views of his touring companions instead of speaking about the strict two-man duel that most of the tennis-watching public sees any Borg v McEnroe match as being.

The trading off of points against abuse sometimes appears to be almost as much a part of McEnroe's technique as his serve or top-spin lob. Docked points are now so common that he often makes less fuss about them than the spectators who call for his blood. Early in Wimbledon 1981, after telling the linesman that he thought he was doing a lousy job, fuming at the foot of the umpire's chair and being penalised for his pains, McEnroe got on with the game and won. The following day sportswriters were demanding that he be flung out of the tournament—one even suggesting that McEnroe's tactics put the very survival of the game in jeopardy and another expressing the certainty that tennis-playing youngsters all over the country would soon be emulating his behaviour.

This is alarmist and unnecessary stuff. McEnroe misbehaves, pays the price and gets on with the game—until the next uproar. It is part of his approach to matches and on the whole he does not bear grudges. The commentators and public will not, however, forgive him and his ill-timed and ill-chosen remarks are emblazoned for public disapproval all over the tabloids after each match. As he has often remarked, it's a pity that microphones for broadcasting purposes pick up his utterances and disgruntled comments, recording them only too loud and clear for viewers. Years ago Billie Jean King (or Moffitt, as she was then), was similarly castigated for her abusive language but, like McEnroe, swore she was only talking to herself. Of disputed calls, a spokesman for the BBC has commented about the fact that whereas in a *Match of the Day* report of a football match a bit of controversial refereeing will be scrutinised and sometimes criticised, this rarely happens in tennis coverage. 'We don't make a great issue of it. Unlike soccer we don't look at a situation and ask "Was the decision right or wrong?" If we replayed every disputed call and incident the judges would be made to look idiots. We must maintain the flow of play.'

This being so, the television viewer must often rely on his or her own impression of events, tempered both by the players' responses and the interpretation from journalist or commentator. In McEnroe's case, where somewhat partial television coverage is not unknown and where opportunities to deplore his manners are seldom missed, the viewer is likely to get the impression that McEnroe will complain without any justification much of the time. This, together with the clear relaying of what might have been a quiet mutter on court tends to help blacken the McEnroe image. This is not to excuse many of the things he says and does on court but to show how their significance can sometimes be distorted.

It is worth remembering that in the Colgate Masters match in 1979, when Connors retired with a painful foot and Mac won on a technical knockout, McEnroe said 'I would rather have finished him off, but beating him . . . I would have it any way I could get it.' Now that is the *real* needle, a more genuine and outward-directed aggression than the boorish asides to linesmen or displays of wounded pride to umpires. Connors had said that he had come to play, not to mess around or quit but there was a note of query in McEnroe's comment that Jimmy's blister hadn't seemed to bother him any in the first set.

Before that match Arthur Ashe said, 'McEnroe is like Connors in that he can hit the ball on the rise, but I don't think he has the best of Connors yet.' Connors had remarked that he thought Mac had to start justifying his reputation and acknowledged that their match was the equivalent of a heavyweight boxing title. At that point he'd beaten McEnroe all four times they'd met, and the atmosphere in which the match was fought was all grudge and grit despite the flower-bedecked court at Madison Square. On the whole, though, McEnroe is liked well enough by his fellow pros. They call him Junior. But with Connors things are different and with the spectators rooting that night for Jimmy and the uneasy relationship between the two men it was an example of McEnroe's most genuinely felt hostility. In a match like that he is not simply fighting to win a game of tennis, but with almost everyone around the place being staunchly ranked against him, he has nothing to lose by verbal aggression, least of all friends.

In May 1979, after he had beaten Borg in four sets in the WCT final, Bjorn said of McEnroe, 'John doesn't have any weaknesses. He has a tremendous touch and feel for the ball. He has reached parity with Connors and myself. Most of the big titles will be between us now.' Why is it that saying this of someone who has just beaten you 7-5, 4-6, 6-2, 7-6, sounds faintly patronising? Perhaps because even the top tennis fraternity recognise that McEnroe is not quite one of them. Certainly not one of the lads. McEnroe had already beaten Borg more than once, and for all its apparent generosity Borg's statement smacks of lordly back-patting and a slightly smug invitation for little Johnny to move up a class. It still does not seem to really recognise a serious threat to his majesty or to demonstrate much in the way of personal warmth. McEnroe's remarks after the same match, when the score between the two men stood at three matches to Borg and two to himself, displayed no arrogance at all. Merely, if anything, collusion with the notion that he hadn't quite made the club.

'Any time I can beat Borg and Connors in the same tournament has to be pretty satisfying but I still rate Bjorn as number one. I'm still 2-6 down to Connors in eight matches, so I can't say I have his number.'

Fellow pro, Roscoe Tanner said at roughly the same time: 'He hits the ball harder and volleys better than Borg and his serve is more deceptive. He moves around the court better than Connors and he can play anywhere on the court.' Mac had several major victories tucked under his headband and with no major tantrums on record for some time and the most consistently positive press coverage of any period since the start of his career, one might wonder why McEnroe went on to compound the Superbrat image instead of sloughing it away.

This was a pivotal time for him. He had begun to win the big ones. He was more than a contender, he was the pretender. Yet after all that McEnroe shocked us all by falling, metaphorically flat on his potato face at Wimbledon that year—beaten in the fourth round by Gullikson. If ever there had been an opportunity to scrape up some sympathy and support this was it but McEnroe did not capitalise. It seems that as his competence grew his popularity, always fragile, shrank again. Whether it is because he actually thrives on animosity or because people resent him for winning, or a mixture of both, is debatable. In any case, over the next few years he became, to use his own phrase, 'the pits of the world', and just as surely his technique improved.

Much has been made of McEnroe's manner. He claims that his lack of popularity does not upset him. But one indiscreet chauffeur told tales of a sniffling Mac grizzling to himself all the way back to his hotel after a particularly unfriendly reception. McEnroe himself, publicly at least, expresses a vehement 'take me or leave me' attitude. It's as if he's given up trying to be understood. 'I don't care if I don't smile on court. Okay I make faces. The faces are me. The people pay to watch me play, and if they want to boo me, that's fine. Let's put it this way. I'd rather get some attention than no attention. If it's bad, that's life!'

A powerful return. McEnroe in action, Stella Artois championships at Queen's Club, 1980

(B) McEnroe in play against Kevin Curren (SA), Wimbledon 1980.
(Keystone Press Agency)

Potato face, Prince Charmless, Superbrat: he claims it's all the same to him so long as he wins. Perhaps this is true and perhaps not. Perhaps he will change. Perhaps not. And perhaps the people who've said he could be one of tennis's all-time greats if only he'd button his lip should consider more often and more seriously the notion that abrasive tension, a physical and intellectual state of barely controlled eruption and a back-against-the-wall dogmatism is one of the key elements of his game and one of the factors that produces the tennis they so unreservedly admire.

McEnroe's low boiling point is not to be admired let alone emulated, but there are a number of characteristics of his game that the average player could do worse than consider. There are the generalisations: the killer instinct, the apparent immunisation from panic when the going gets very rough indeed, the speed, the fierce and intimidating way that all this can unnerve an opponent. The concentration, the range of shots and the way he angles them. He doesn't freeze at matchpoint but seizes the moment and moves in for the kill where another player might become tentative. His flexibility and ease of movement and his command of the whole court are all exceptional.

Following an almost magically placed racket head McEnroe will move into any shot with perfectly paced elegance. The racket head will usually get there first: when other players return 'impossible' shots one is often more aware of their feat than one is when watching McEnroe because he rarely scrambles, rarely appears to win a point by fluke. The racket leads, the body follows imperceptibly afterwards. In this he is much like Borg who has said that McEnroe has 'radar eyes.'

THE SERVE

A few years ago male tennis players tended to be judged by the speed of their serve. Tennis in the mid to late sixties was actually less interesting than it is today because more subtlety has returned to the game and the 6-1, 6-0, 6-2 result

100

is less likely these days. McEnroe's serve is certainly one of his greatest strengths but it is not among the most savagely fast in the game. It's been compared, in its action, to a slowly unwinding cobra which extends its awesome neck for the kill. Doubles partner Fleming calls him 'Snakey'. McEnroe has an exceptional record for aces—the serves which are virtually unplayable, let alone returnable. One reason for this is variety. He doesn't have one set piece but a number of ways of directing it so that the man at the other end of the court, rocking from foot to foot and blowing on his fingers has to keep guessing. His ability to alter the speed, spin and placement of the ball is one of the most dangerous aspects of his game. The serve starts with that high, slow toss, and unorthodox but oddly graceful beginning. The racket is low —McEnroe characteristically dips almost to his ankles and pitches the ball carefully like a recreation ground beginner. The ball is thrown just high enough for maximum impact when the racket is drawn up to strike it. Every McEnroe serve seems to be made in slow-motion, yet somehow the next thing you hear is '15-love'. The advantage of being left-handed means that his spin breaks in the opposite direction of a right-hander, which can ruffle opponents.

McEnroe does not make a habit of bounding forward to the net, possibly because his serve is so frequently good that it would be an unnecessary journey. Even his second serve is often as forceful as many players' first. But if he needs to be at the net he'll be ready to make that light, wristy shot that skims the net, bounces and darts diagonally out of court before the other chap has had time to race forward for the return. His smallish build—especially in the last year or so —again gives the lie that it takes a big man to serve consistent winners.

RETURN OF SERVICE

When he's at the receiving end of another man's serve McEnroe has a wide vocabulary of answers. When faced with a hard serve McEnroe rarely follows the conventional procedure of a hefty backswing. In a deceptively gentle way he tends to merely block the ball by extending the racket, making perfectly placed contact and guiding the ball surely back to the most inaccessible spot on the other side of the net. In this way he wastes neither energy or time. McEnroe utilises, in fact, the ready-made power that exists in an aggressive serve and simply deflects it. Basically it is the karate principle of turning the other man's force back upon himself. Economy and intelligence. It seems obvious—but how often have you seen someone save an apparently lost point with a magnificently if strenuously executed return, only to lose the next point (one that might look easy), because they were in the wrong place and still gasping from their heroic return? The key to this is anticipation, which is hard to learn. Knowing where and how to return that service is partly instinct. Typically McEnroe will send back thudding winners simply by extending an arm. The other man's racket will be flailing several feet beyond the chalk whilst the McEnroe ball has plopped just an inch or two inside.

THE VOLLEY

McEnroe's volley is exquisite. He has the ability to make his opponent hustle and rush, appear almost clumsy and wrong-footed. If his serve is like a languid snake his volley is one of the most graceful and elegant sights in tennis today, and just as venomous. Again, the breadth of his range is an important part of his success with this shot. A high ball —one that is pitched towards his shoulder will be met and driven back because McEnroe has placed his feet and bent the knees for maximum accuracy and aim. The low ball—those conventionally unreachable drop shots that arrive near the ankles will be flipped arrogantly over the net only to trickle unplayably away. Another example of McEnroe utilising the character of the shot he is receiving: if he takes a soft, powerless shot he will return it with only sufficient force to dip it over the net. Not enough for it to bounce and be returned. Sounds simple, but to tackle a ball like that without unnecessary force—effort that could make it returnable—the player needs to be perfectly positioned. Anticipation again.

McEnroe tends to keep his body and his racket head well apart. The knees are bent, the racket extended sideways, perfect balance, perfect footwork and a hawk eye for the ball are all techniques which can be practised. Once again the wrists work hard. The entire strength of the torso, through arm to wrist, can go into one of these shots. If he has had to reach for the ball the force of the last stride seems to be charged into the movement. After playing a typical volley, with his weight poised now on the front foot and the ball tearing to its target, McEnroe is ready for the return. He tends not to alter position now, rather waiting to see where the speed of the return will take him next. There is a stillness in his play, closely linked with his speed, that allows him to pause for a crucial moment between shots. He fidgets a lot while awaiting serve, but seldom otherwise. He is incredibly fast, but rarely looks hurried.

Despite the wisdom of the manuals and of many coaches, McEnroe takes the time to relax the racket between volleys. His confidence in his touch allows him to play an audacious game. The key points to watch are the short swing, a crisp groundstroke jab with little bodily follow-through which works—and this is the most difficult part to achieve —when ball hits gut dead centre. Having placed the ball correctly, a very tight grip on impact ensures a more powerful volley and it is important to be 'under the ball' for the classic forehand. Champions use firm, short strokes which fly solidly over the net. The thrust is important, but as for placing—that is less easily described. Practice obviously makes better, if not perfect. The experts say that the most tricky positions to volley from are the right hip of the right hander and the left hip of the sinister.

GROUND STROKES

Co-ordination is the key to successful ground-strokes. Being fast is one of McEnroe's stocks in trade and this, like most other court skills, comes from peak physical condition and well developed anticipation and reflexes. The whole body needs to be well co-ordinated. The eye, the hand, the feet and legs and that further, near miraculous telepathy between body and racket. When McEnroe has pulled wide for a shot, with his left leg typically bent and raised and his body tilting sideways to the net, he will arrive perfectly balanced to meet the ball. His physical strength has quite often been metered out in the run to reach the ball. Once he's there he will play with economical effort and it won't always look like a big deal. He rarely takes a big swing but will still glance the ball back with deceptive speed. This is where timing is important. The racket head in full momentum and the strings placed correctly against the ball for spin and the aim of his return will often make it unplayable. It is generally thought that in these shots McEnroe has a more consistent mastery than most other players. He's got all the angles. He calls the shots. This is principally due to his perfected and impeccable timing and his inter-shot speed. The result is a kind of graceful, gliding cross-court pass that makes even his harshest critics gasp.

Back Hand

Unlike Jimmy Connors or Bjorn Borg (one grunts, the other doesn't) with their famous double-fisted backhands, John McEnroe has not made a speciality of his backhand. When called upon to use it he can bring all his usual speed and elegance and, ironically for his opponents, it is surprising how often a set or match has been decided on a backhand winner from Mac. But the shot is not in his regular vocabulary of blinders, partly because his court speed often enables him to get into position to play a forehand. If it were actually a weakness in his game we would know much more about it and other players would have exploited it. As it is, he approaches backhand shots with conventional and professional competence rather than with the unorthodox imagination he brings to other aspects of his game.

McEnroe's speed really is worth a note to itself. It has been said that he is faster around the court that anyone else on the circuit. He is a glider and a pouncer. Arthur Ashe has said that you can always tell a glider by the state of their socks after a match on clay. If they're grubby it's clear their owner has had to scramble and scrape to meet the shots. The smooth, fast footwork are honed through the best practice of all—top level matches. However, anyone who plays soccer as well as tennis has a built-in advantage as the dribbling and turning techniques which are part of soccer training come in very handy for speed on the tennis court. McEnroe, of course, played soccer at school. Quick movements, reactions, the ability to turn and thrust without losing balance and the containment of these manoeuvres to the ankles and legs, leaving the shoulders and arms free and strong to fire off a winner is exemplified by watching soccer training. Players dribble rapidly with arms balanced loose at their sides and shoulders drooping.

DOUBLES

A precis of points is given here as the chapter on doubles play covers much of the technical expertise that McEnroe brings to the game. Doubles matches utilise McEnroe's amazing speed and reflexes to the full since doubles are generally faster, more breathless matches than singles, calling for the highest level of anticipation and net skills. Peter Fleming and McEnroe are well-matched partners. Indeed McEnroe was a doubles champion long before he won a major singles title. Although superficially it is the strength of McEnroe that has pulled off titles for this pair, the tennis relationship of Fleming and Mac is like many a good marriage—a sympathetic fusion of contrasts if not opposites. Their play is a duet of overwhelming force . . . the McEnroe serve and Fleming's excellence in the tramlines.

McEnroe's neat and nifty speed is matched by the reach and subtlety of Fleming. Between them they are terrifically fast at the net.

As a team they work well: fond of and in tune with each other, generous (this is essential for a good doubles relationship) and intuitive. They've played together long enough to understand each other's play and responses. They present an impressive serve and volley attack and employ a rare understanding of their other half's sense of geography. One will be fairly sure of the other's position on court at any time, so their play lacks the 'nannying' that has marked other doubles partnerships. It leaves them free to play with delicate manoeuvres, strategies and double-bluffs in much the same way as two people who have played bridge together for years can form a winning team.

PSYCHOLOGICAL WARFARE

It has been said that McEnroe intimidates anyone who happens to be around the court—players, officials and spectators. That he tries to bludgeon others into accepting his version of events. It may be this is deliberate gamesmanship, but he denies it and I tend to believe him. His father has said that John only gets angry when he feels a genuine error has been made. McEnroe has strong feelings about officials and the way in which they perform. Some years ago an elderly line judge fell asleep during a match at Wimbledon and one hesitates to imagine how McEnroe would have responded if he had been on court at the time. Officials are fallible but McEnroe will not tolerate mistakes. He is not a fool. He knows perfectly well that he is unlikely to be able to change an umpire's decision. Squabbles are seldom to his direct advantage. So his fights are usually foolish and pointless —except to McEnroe who is taking issue on principle. The officials are not usually frightened into giving in.

As for the idea that he intimidates his opponent: I find this hard to accept. Players on the professional circuit are unlikely to be sheltered, over-sensitive or susceptible to the notion that McEnroe is out to personally humiliate them. He is out to win, but tends only to make issues if he feels he is absolutely right. He has an element of generosity in his make-up that seems to preclude knowingly spiteful arguments or wrangles for wrangles' sake. It is unlikely that he knowingly attempts to disturb the other person's concentration although he must realise that this happens, so it may be selfish of him to sustain these fights just for the sake of speaking his mind.

His own game was destroyed by a particularly big fight when he met Jimmy Connors in the Benson and Hedges final in 1981, and it could be mentioned here that if anyone in that match appeared to knowingly and cynically capitalise on the disturbance, it was Connors. McEnroe may be his own worst enemy and a thoughtless emotional hooligan, but a devious manipulator he is almost certainly not. The only sense in which he is sinister is that he is left-handed. John McEnroe has much to teach other players at almost any other level but no-one would be wise to copy his manners. They can only harm. It is only through the quality of his game that McEnroe has become a winner, not by thought-out gamesmanship. Many other players, as well as the Mayer brothers, would have complained if it was. Ludicrous and alarmist accusations that his behaviour will lead to bad manners on every tennis court, in every school and club in the land are misjudged indeed. How often has McEnroe been seen to benefit from the rows? And who in Britain would complain if we produced a player here of such talent and such temperament? I do wish he'd learn to stop flogging a dead horse and to develop one or two basic notions of diplomacy, and remember that he gets some lucky calls too. It's all part of the game, and he's benefited from imperfect line calls now and again.

Tennis, its rules and regulators will probably change a bit but it will take time for the game to become as perfectly seamed as McEnroe would like. His little brother could have hung up his Nikes before that day comes. In the meantime Mac might just as well accept the fallibilities of the game and those who officiate. They are human too. If he can't he might just as well change to another game. Space Invaders, for instance . . .

On balance I admire his anger because it is from this spirit that such tremendous play is derived—the play that has entranced his most vigilant critics. It is also this mindless, pointless, undisciplined emotion that makes him query the sometimes curious logic and rules of tennis. But above all it is by this that he demonstrates to the public that he is a person. The edges are still very rough, McEnroe is still young. I hope, for the sake of his professional success that he will manage to plane smooth some of his more abrasive edges. But I dread the time that he becomes a playboy, an automaton or a tennis lobotomy.

Wimbledon, 1981. Faces of frustration.
(Photos: Ken Saunders/The Guardian)

7

FOR A FEW DOLLARS MORE

He's one of the greatest guys I know   *Peter Fleming*

He doesn't go out of his way to impress people   *Mary Carillo*

Devastating   *Frew McMillan*

For a start doubles is a lot more fun*

Sandy Mayer is the biggest cry baby on the circuit   *Peter Fleming*

When I'm playing singles and there's something wrong, I often find I can work it out in doubles*

I have been playing crap for a year, dragging us down, but Junior insists it's his fault as well. We're a team   *Peter Fleming*

Sometimes I think they are unfair to McEnroe *Mike Davies*, former British Davis Cup player

Often when McEnroe seethes and fumes at the foot of the umpire's ladder viewers are left

with only one side of the argument. They see
the effect of the argument but not the *cause*
  John Sadler

If he was beaten in a singles match he'd try
even harder in the doubles   *Peter Fleming*

Our friendship is more important than winning
or losing   *Peter Fleming*

We win two-thirds of the matches without even
trying, for godsakes*

* John McEnroe

In the furore that almost invariably attends his singles
matches, it is sometimes easy to overlook the fact that
McEnroe is a brilliant and successful doubles player too. A
former, current and very likely future Wimbledon champion
in the doubles, McEnroe had his first major successes playing
such matches. Doubles partnerships tend to be durable—one
thinks of Bob Hewitt and Frew McMillan, of Tony Roche
and John Newcombe. They are sometimes apparently mismatched combinations such as Ilie Nastase (then at the height
of his brilliance and success) and Connors (at the time the
rorty, unsophisticated cub). Occasionally the team goes on to
become fondly regarded as old war horses who'll play a
reliable game well into their thirties: rarely absolutely scintillating but terrifically competent and enjoyable to watch, like
Stan Smith and Bob Lutz.
    A factor that marks the great doubles partnerships is the
fierce loyalty that can exist between the pair. Sometimes one
half seems to be the better player by a stretch of astro-turf,
the match turning on the power of the stronger serve, the
quicker return. But just as it takes two people to make
scintillating conversation, even if one of the protagonists is
the inspirational half and the other simply supplies splendid

repartee, there is really no such thing as a passenger in great doubles. The success of McEnroe and Peter Fleming has sometimes been too strictly attributed to Mac with Fleming's failure to excel in singles cited as evidence. But there have always been players who have a particular genius for doubles, for whom it has not been a poor second to singles glory and whose real home has been in the tramlines.

Peter Fleming, known as 'Flam' on the pro-circuit, may be such a player, although it should not be forgotten that on the circuit he does a consistent fair to middling job in singles. He's been known to beat McEnroe once in a while—as in the semi-finals of the Italian indoor championships when he beat Mac 6-4, 6-1. He has been graceful about the shadow that his partner has sometimes appeared to cast upon him. The fact is that McEnroe is twice-gifted: although clearly concentrating on singles, he has a natural ease and instinct that has made him—with Fleming—one of the great doubles players too. He won his first Wimbledon title with Fleming in the doubles in 1979 when they beat Brian Gottfried and Raul Ramirez 4-6, 6-4, 6-2, 6-2 in two hours and ten minutes.

Seeded No. 1, it was a result that surprised no-one although the veterans Hewitt and McMillan were also taking part. Earlier that year he and Fleming had won the Braniff Airways world doubles title at Olympia in London, but McEnroe told Barry Newcombe that he wouldn't consider that he had 'arrived' as a player until he started to win titles at Wimbledon or at the French or US Opens. At that point he and Fleming had been playing together for about two years although their closeness gives the impression of a longer friendship. Both are New Yorkers, Fleming being three years older than McEnroe. He was at UCLA before playing full-time. Neither shows much exuberance on court, Fleming sometimes seeming nervy and deceptively tentative. His serve, whilst not in the McEnroe class, is usually strong since doubles partnerships are often a combination of rocket serve and nifty, delicate net play. Peter Fleming at 6 ft 5 ins, has the advantage of enormous reach.

It is a joy to watch doubles at its best—a combination of force, imagination, speed and an occasional hilarity which is rare in singles matches. Characterised as good doubles are by intuition and sympathy, it is inevitable that mistakes and muddles sometimes occur. These often, though seldom in the case of Mac and Fleming, lead to laughter and goodwill on both sides of the net and off court too. It is perhaps because of this human element that doubles have rarely been regarded quite as seriously as singles matches, and why mixed doubles get very little intense scrutiny.

With their Home Counties tennis club, knockabout feel, the mixed doubles has always been something of an anti-climax at Wimbledon. Until recently it was played after the men's final on Saturday afternoon, and after most of the day's tension had been discharged. The boys and girls came out and gave a good natured display and a cheerful memory for the crowd to take home in between savouring the moments of higher drama earlier in the afternoon. For the players involved it is doubtless important to win. But somehow even they do not seem to invest such energy into this festive finale of the finals.

McEnroe's former mixed doubles partner, Mary Carillo, with whom he came to Wimbledon in 1977 after winning the mixed doubles at the French Open, has said that McEnroe tended to bring an unusual intensity to these matches. She says he has no subtlety of emotion. 'He doesn't go out of his way to impress people. He just doesn't care what people think. The game is so simple for him and he just gets mad when anything goes wrong.' Perhaps because he is so temperamentally unsuited to the languid, good-natured spirit that mixed doubles are often played in, McEnroe no longer makes this event part of his tournament repertoire.

Whilst not quite sharing the dour determination of his partner, Peter Fleming takes his game very seriously indeed, although he has leavened potentially spiky interviews after matches by a more relaxed attitude and a disarming realism about his partner. After the 1979 final in which a couple of dicey line calls were violently disputed by McEnroe, journalists asked Mac how he would tackle Borg if they were ever to meet in the final. He would attack, said McEnroe. 'Where?' asked the press. 'At the changeover,' replied Fleming. At this McEnroe, like everyone else present, dissolved helplessly into laughter.

Fleming and McEnroe got to know each other well during the early years of their partnership by sharing both hotel rooms and a common branding as pugnacious youngsters. Fleming, however, has rarely shown such controversial manners as his partner. 'I guess I always had too much Irish in me,' was McEnroe's defence to enquiries about his habit of spitting. Now this might seem unfair to the Irish who, as a race, are known for a variety of talents and a host of different vices. However, it did not deter the Irish international footballer who gave McEnroe his number three shirt after the 1981 final. McEnroe was wearing it shortly afterwards.

Fleming and McEnroe, whatever other people might think, regard each other as equals and as between all equals, violent exchanges occasionally occur. After a quarrel on court when they were playing against each other in Jamaica, Fleming let rip 'Just because I'm your friend doesn't mean I'm the Salvation Army,' he said. The two did not speak to each other for days. Eventually they talked it out over a couple of drinks by the pool and it transpired that what had really upset McEnroe was not the original issue but the fact that Fleming had yelled at him. It's odd that such a tender and easily bruised sensitivity doesn't see that other people can be similarly wounded by his own stormy outbursts.

'The problem is that on court he thinks only about winning the next point. Nothing else counts,' said Fleming. McEnroe's temper is easily roused and can be sustained over the course of a set or a match. But he does not hold onto grudges and if he appears to be boorish or ungenerous it is far more likely to be the result of defensive dismay at other people's judgements of him than of continuing anger.

Fleming has often been asked to explain his partner's behaviour and to give instant psychoanalysis. He's naturally wary of this but has said many times that John is misunderstood. According to Fleming, Mac is a sort of Jekyll and Hyde figure, very different off court from on and unruly behaviour in matches is simply intense competitiveness. 'It gives people the impression that he's a real sourpuss . . . but believe me there are a hell of a lot of players who are twice as dodgy as John on the circuit, fellas I wouldn't be associated with. John is trying to clean up his image, but remember he is very young and has a lot to learn about living.' Fleming sees the root of the image problems as the surprise appearance in the Wimbledon semi-finals in 1977.

'He couldn't handle the publicity and all the pressure because he was only seventeen. So the press gave him a bad time, he resented what they'd written and so it went on. John has improved but he's been given little credit for it.' The sparring with journalists has continued and by 1981 McEnroe was convinced, with a sureness bordering on a persecution complex, that there was a Fleet Street conspiracy to blacken his name.

Fleming drew an interesting comparison with Nastase, saying that the Rumanian is the same in the locker room as he is on court—always moaning about something and trying to upset people. The public and press, said Fleming, are usually ready to forgive Nastase, but the players are sick to death with the antics. According to Fleming the other players on the circuit respect John and do not join in the general badmouthing. There are exceptions. Of Sandy Mayer, whom Fleming and Mac played (with Mayer's brother Gene) at an invitational tournament at Forest Hills in 1979, Fleming said, 'Sandy Mayer is the biggest cry-baby on the circuit. Let's get that straight.' It had been a needle match, with the Mayers complaining to the umpire that McEnroe had been deliberately distracting their service games by swinging his racket when Fleming was about to face serve. Then Sandy Mayer had commented that McEnroe wasted time between games. Mayer has made many remarks about McEnroe.

'Look at the time he stops to tie up his shoe-laces —almost always before a big point. I'd be perfectly willing to tie his laces before a match and I guarantee they'd stay tied.' This kind of complaint about Mac is not common from players. Of the racket-swinging shock horror McEnroe said after the match (which the Mayers won 6-4, 2-6, 7-6), that he had not intended to irritate or distract.

The Wimbledon doubles success of 1979 had been preceded by the lifting of the Braniff title—their sixth doubles in the eight months since McEnroe had turned pro. Mac was now rated fifth in the world in singles and, with Fleming, third in doubles. The still rather chubby McEnroe and the lanky Fleming were a familiar sight on the world grand prix map. McEnroe spoke of his attitude to doubles at the time.

'For a start it's a lot of fun. There's not the same pressure. I always find that a lot of the time when I'm playing singles and there's something wrong, I can work it out in doubles.' He also spoke of the importance, at that stage of his career, of 'getting matches in,' of the need to gain court experience at the highest level and to take all the opportunities he could to test his skills against some of the players he hoped to confound before long on the singles court. Most of the world's top players—Connors, Borg, Gerulaitis and Vilas to name only some—shun doubles play, feeling possibly that it dilutes their energies and that a doubles title is not prestigious enough to be worth the effort. It is likely that McEnroe's attitude helped him to improve to the extent that two years after turning pro, he was ranked three in the world.

Athough he is more relaxed about doubles and it seems to give him marginally more pleasure than singles, McEnroe is earnest and serious about his matches with Fleming. Doubles, after all, taught him to be a champion long before singles ever did. The number of matches he plays on clay might help him to win the French Open one day. It's premature to suggest that success on the clay of Paris eludes McEnroe in much the same was as Flushing Meadow jinxes Borg, but with a record of withdrawals and early defeats there, McEnroe might be beginning to fear that he'll never achieve in France what he has achieved at home and in Britain.

'Devastating,' was how McMillan and Hewitt described McEnroe and Fleming at the Braniff championships.* The new boys had improved enormously since they had beaten them in the doubles final of the previous Wimbledon. After the Braniff final McEnroe denied that money was an incentive for winning matches. 'I've got quite enough of that already.' Winning was what really mattered. With his lugubrious-faced blond partner he began a long and lucky

* That year the success/failure ratio in McEnroe-Fleming doubles matches stood at an astounding 69 to 3.

Faces of frustration.

(Photos: Ken Saunders/The Guardian)

streak in doubles play, but their path hit some bad rocks after Wimbledon 1979 and as McEnroe's singles star has ascended, his doubles fortunes have become more variable.

It is worth noting that in a smallish tournament in 1979, the Jack Kramer Open in Los Angeles, McEnroe went down to Fleming in the final. It was a match marked by an unusual number of disputes including a five-minute delay on two occasions when McEnroe (seeded No. 1 as reigning US Open champion), refused to resume play after first protesting about a service call and later about boisterous audience participation. His ankle had been being giving him trouble, but after his 6-4, 6-4 defeat by Fleming he blamed, uncharacteristically, the unsettling calls for his failure. However, possibly the most interesting aspect of this match was his behaviour towards a spectator who had narrowly missed being struck by his racket after he let go of it in a doomed, flying effort to race to a cross court shot. After the match he apologised to the spectator and gave her his racket.

Fleming and McEnroe had hit a tough patch by 1980. By May, McEnroe was in the middle of a long run of singles defeats (three by Connors, three by Gerulaitis, twice by Vilas and by Harold Soloman and Jose Luis Clerc one apiece). His doubles form was also suffering and the pair were failing to retain their grip. At Wimbledon, after his punishing semi-final victory against Connors, McEnroe was unable to give Fleming his usual support and they went out to Australians McNamee and McNamara by 6-3, 6-2, 6-3. Fleming, as usual was generous. 'I have been playing crap for a year, dragging us down, but Junior insists it's his fault as well. We're a team.' British audiences, fed on anti-brat publicity by now and pleased, possibly, to see the Davis Cup rout vicariously revenged, showed no marked dismay. Other players had the odd comment on McEnroe's flagging form. Gerulaitis said he'd been playing too much, that all those ten hour flights and long matches when he hadn't been really fit had taken their toll. McEnroe himself, although mindful of the old ankle injury, said that he wanted to avoid making excuses for himself. He recognised, painfully, the lapses and blamed himself for not pushing himself harder.

'You hope you are perfect all the time but that is

118

impossible and the true champion is the guy who can play when he is not 100 per cent.' He agreed that he probably had played too much recently but said that the most difficult thing to do was say 'No' to a series which he felt could be useful to play in. McEnroe's intolerance is legendary, but he seems least tolerant of all of his own short-comings and limitations. Unwilling to offer routine excuses like physical injury or exhaustion, he continued to push himself beyond match-winning form.

The stress of their continuing disappointments took its toll on Fleming, too. He was subject to warnings in his own singles matches. After a points deduction at Wimbledon he said, 'It was the attitude of the umpire in my match which is the main cause of the problems McEnroe suffers from. They refuse to acknowledge things, they're inflexible and if you ask them a question their only response is "15-love". There is nothing more frustrating. They should treat us like human beings.' In another match Fleming was in trouble early on and made a series of sarcastic comments to the umpire about the net cord judge. Finally, when he was allowed a let he cried 'Eureka! He's got it right.' Umpire Maurice Jacobs applied a penalty point for this unseemly mocking and his ruling was upheld by the referee who had been sent for at Fleming's request.

So the slogging all over the world to play in tournaments large and small—and, let it be remembered, for large sums of money—was imposing a deep strain on both Fleming and McEnroe after their early *blitz krieg* of the doubles circuit. Both as individuals and as a team their game suffered and although they climbed steadily back to form in 1981 (despite some slightly lip-smacking predictions that they were a burnt out case) and went on to take the Wimbledon doubles title, their future as a team does not seem so assured as it did when McEnroe was on his early steep ascendant.

Now that he has reached the peaks it may be that he will play doubles with less commitment, joining Borg, Connors and the rest of the first division in his single-minded devotion to the classic two-man duel. This would be a great loss for the tennis-watching public and something approaching disaster for Fleming whose greatest moments of glory are seldom seen on the singles court. It is unlikely that McEnroe will completely ditch doubles, but certainly these days he has less need of the experience and training that such matches offer. On the other hand he has even more need of their restorative, relaxing atmosphere.

I would like to think that in ten or twelve years time, when McEnroe has, inevitably, ceded his singles mastery to a new, younger man, that there will still be the pleasure of watching him and Fleming battling it out on the doubles court à la Smith, Lutz, Hewitt, McMillan, Newcombe and Roche. They could show a pair of brash youngsters just what the old stagers can pull out of their bag of tricks and experience. I'd like to see them making that stately walk over to the Duchess of Kent to collect the doubles trophy and cheque. It's an entertaining whimsy to wonder whether then at last McEnroe, with Fleming, will be afforded the kind of affectionate respect that the intervening years of great, value-for-money tennis will have earned him. Or perhaps he will still be grim-faced and awkward, shout just as often at officials and be, by tennis standards, an elderly reprobate.

Either way is good enough. The Fleming-McEnroe partnership, surviving as it has the most stressed and difficult period of McEnroe's professional life to come back and capture the 1981 Wimbledon crown, is a delight of skills, grace and intuition. The mutual respect and generosity which each man shows the other indicates a lasting friendship, so perhaps we can hope for another ten years or so of tempestuous, variable, inspirational and always interesting tennis. And perhaps it will be on this court, if no other, that one day McEnroe will feel the warmth he has missed and the respect he deserves.

8

DAYS OF WHINES AND RAGES

I think he's charming. He's a pet *Judith Craig, sculptress*

He's kind, attentive and gentle *Stacy Margolin*

I've got a nice girlfriend*

I'm not complaining about this fame thing, but it's hard to grasp. I feel like a normal kid*

He never shut his mouth till the food dripped out *Robert Polhemus, Stanford University*

The classic example of the hysterical extrovert *Daily Express*

He doesn't need groupies. I'm his only girl *Stacy Margolin*

Not everyone should be like McEnroe but not everyone should be like Borg either. All McEnroe does is complain. Does he kill anyone? What does he do that is so horrible? *Ilie Nastase*

I think I get on alright with the other players
now. I think they've accepted me*

A teenager no more. No more a teenaged hero.
Yeah. Great*

You hope you are perfect all the time but that
is impossible*

On the fifteen minute journey he fiddled with
the radio, rubbed his chin, picked his spots but
didn't say a word   *Daily Mirror*

Whatever McEnroe lacks in charm he certainly
has in courage   *Daily Mail*

Tennis is a great sport and if it's going to survive it's not going to do so by supressing personality. If you do you'll have robots on the court
in ten years*

There are so many rules I don't think anyone
knows the rules. It's unbelievable*

I didn't see any journalists*   [*on leaving Heathrow, July 1981*]

He has no subtlety   *Mary Carillo*

He has no sense of humour   *Ilie Nastase*

Hell, you have to stand up for your rights*

He's greedy, selfish, arrogant, vulgar, self-
interested and cheap   *Nicholas Fairbairn, Solic-
iter General for Scotland, in the Daily
Telegraph.*

You need time alone and time to think. It's not
exactly fun to lie on some bed in your room
and watch TV between practice and playing but
that's the way I want it.*

* *John McEnroe*

In a grittily perceptive boxed featurette, the medical correspondent of the *Daily Express*, John Stevenson, analysed 'the mind of Superyob'. The need to keep up concentration, observed Mr. Stevenson, is the main factor influencing McEnroe's behaviour. When facing an opponent of equal or superior ability—Borg for instance—Superyob finds he does not need to raise the cloven hoof, but with less challenging opposition McEnroe can easily become bored and thus shouts abuse in order to maintain his interest in the game. This is, I think, the essence of the *Express*'s interpretation of current psycholanalytical opinion. In the view of shrinks who have studied McEnroe (one wonders whether a new medical condition, McEnroe's Syndrome, perhaps, will emerge as a result), he is the classic example of the hysterical extrovert who needs to manufacture anger to ward off boredom.

Insults, rudeness and other devices are used to produce adrenalin. Dougal Mackay, principal clinical psychologist at St. Mary's Hospital, London, is quoted as saying 'Every top competitor needs to get the adrenalin going in order to get a performance to its peak. If he [McEnroe] knows he can beat someone of lesser calibre, then his biggest risk is boredom.' This searching article appeared the day the nation was rocking on its heels and spluttering on its gin and tonics because McEnroe had addressed someone as 'the pits of the world.' Incidentally it is not known if McEnroe's pits were intended to convey an image of armpits (probable), fruit pits (unlikely—the American version of pips or the little hard things you find in the middle of fruit is hardly a bitter enough insult to merit all the fuss), or the pits of depression, gloomy dark places like coal mines (possible: this would concur with some of McEnroe's other picturesque epithets).

Other authorities weighed in after Wimbledon 1981 with explanations of the burning question about McEnroe's behaviour and unpopularity. *Paris Match*, the stylish, gossipy French glossy, wrote after Wimbledon, 'Nobody was surprised by the sour expression of the Duke of Kent when he presented the Cup to the winner. It is impossible to be a prince of the royal blood and to hobnob with such an insolent urchin. You cannot be first cousin to Queen Elizabeth and show esteem for this young Irish American who has dynamited tradition.' *Paris Match* continued in its colourful Gallic way and made tentative links between Mac and the troubles in Northern Ireland. Calling McEnroe a 'provo' it added that 'McEnroe is the stubborn Irishman; a Catholic, a second-generation American . . . and the contempt of certain Englishmen for the Irish goes back centuries.' The British Embassy in the Faubourg St. Honoré replied coolly to *Paris Match*'s assertions. 'This article reveals a lack of understanding of the Irish situation', it announced. Well said, chaps . . . on the other hand I'm not so sure.

Earlier the *Daily Mirror's* august Peter Wilson had written a 'Dear John' open letter to the wayward genius. The message, if somewhat patronising and without startling statement or advice, was reasonably restrained. 'You have the ability to become one of the youngest champions of modern times. . . . There is no doubt of your ability. It's your behaviour on court that upsets me. Play tennis and you'll walk out of Wimbledon a clear winner. But if you lose do so gracefully and the crowds who love the game will applaud you as much in honourable defeat as they would in generous victory.' Apart from, once again, the sense here that somehow McEnroe's first duty is to please the crowd, there is a faint suggestion that Mac does not know how to be a good loser. While he frequently—often wrongly and almost always pointlessly—disputes points and shows a churlish rancour when things don't go his way, McEnroe has never behaved gracelessly or bitterly at the end of a match if he has lost. True, he doesn't generally give the brave devil-may-care smile of fiction's charming losers, or drape his arm around the victor's shoulder to show what good pals they are off court. He usually looks rather sad. After all, he's lost, and he *does* care. But he gives full credit to the winner, makes no excuses for himself and, equally, he seldom shows much more emotion if he does win.

Letters to the newspapers from the reading public during 1981 Wimbledon ranged the spectrum. 'Why should this warrior be shown any mercy? He took no quarter and having won the battle ran away with the banner and left the wounded to hold the fort', wrote a woman from St. Leonards on Sea in

Leaping towards Wimbledon victory, 1981.

(Keystone Press Agency)

a precarious pyramid of military metaphors. 'Unless some-one shows him a little understanding, which doesn't look very likely at the moment, the sad, vicious circle of condem-nation, increased stress and even more anger will never be broken', countered another from Barrow in Suffolk. The St. Leonards's view was the more generally upheld, but Suffolk certainly wasn't a lone voice.

There is a nice side to John McEnroe. It is known, for instance, that he turned down all that money to play in an exhibition in South Africa and played for charity instead. He has had to restrain himself from much more aggravation than most players, particularly at Wimbledon. Chris Evert Lloyd (who wasn't very well-liked at Wimbledon in her first summers but who has recently, especially since her marriage to Englishman John Lloyd, acquired near-regal status) said, 'Wimbledon crowds are strange. If you lose a few matches you seem more human to them. They like you better.' But Mac has lost a few matches at Wimbledon and seems no nearer to public acceptance.

He told Jean Rook, the acerbic Fleet Street columnist, 'I do try to have manners—I'm really working on them, not swearing and all that. Maybe I'm not succeeding so well but I get so angry with myself when I play a bad ball, I show it and there's nothing much I can do about it. People keep saying that I'm nastier that Ilie Nastase but it's a different thing with him. I'm very fond of Ilie but he really does set out to deliberately upset people. I don't copy him, I don't aim to annoy people. I just can't help getting mad with myself . . . but why do people over here go on as if I'd committed some terrible crime like murder or something?

'Sure I like to be praised and liked. Who doesn't? A lot of people say I don't care about anything or anybody but my tennis. I can't argue with writers who say that, but it's just not true. Tennis isn't the end of my world. I do care about my family and friends and I'm an easy-going guy off court.'

Part of McEnroe's problems spring from being a loner. Borg, coincidentally, played badly in Milan in March 1981 where Mac beat him in the final leg of the WCT tour. His Svengali figure, coach Lennart Bergelin was recuperating from an operation and absent. Superdad attends some of his boy's big matches, watching like a hawk-eyed Lee J. Cobb, but McEnroe has no regular companion to take the strain. He has no Marianna offering mute support at the courtside and encouragement back at the hotel. He and Stacy Margolin appear to meet only erratically when their playing schedules will allow. Awaiting serve Mac quivers with energy, rarely showing the still composure that distinguishes some of his rivals. He will twitch, fidget with his shirt and endlessly tighten his shoe-laces between games. And this restlessness is reflected in the amount he works. Perhaps it is sheer greed and he only does it for the money, but McEnroe plays harder than most of the pros on the circuit. Of his absence from a £285,000 tournament in Dubai, open to sixteen players, McEnroe commented, 'You have to be crazy to go there. There's no way I would go. Anyway, I wasn't invited.' From this McEnroe's attitude towards playing for money pure and simple is ambivalent, but already a millionaire, he certainly doesn't need to play where he doesn't wish to go. McEnroe has said that he uses tournaments as practice, especially doubles, but whatever his motives for this punishing schedule, no-one can accuse him of slacking.

McEnroe's battle with his own temper is played on a battleground to some extent prepared by the press, which has sometimes been less than totally generous in its coverage of his victories. It is surprising that he feels ill-served sometimes when the *Daily Telegraph*'s banner headline after his win over Borg in the US Open was *Bold McEnroe denies Borg the Grand Slam he so richly deserves*? The same article concluded that where he'd left the Centre Court at Wimbledon after the final as a 'losing hero' he left Flushing Meadow as a 'winning villain'. Such comments inescapably imply that a McEnroe win is somehow not quite morally right, that a better man has been robbed and McEnroe might well feel peeved if he reads them.

Despite forthright and astonishingly undiplomatic comments about Wimbledon, McEnroe was not among the group of pros who threatened to withdraw from the championships in 1980 because of behind-the-scenes disputes over some of the rules. The rampant pros (who elected to play after all), were also threatening to boycott the US Open. McEnroe said,

'There are many things wrong with both championships, but everyone says they are the best so I guess they must be.' These supportive sentiments were expressed after a drizzly, draughty week at Wimbledon where McEnroe had had anything but a jolly, trouble-free time.

In fact from this incident it could be conjectured that McEnroe quarrels *upfront* with points of order and rules which many of his fellow pros are less openly uneasy about. Whereas they accept the terms on court and play on, mostly without shrieking their despair or disapproval, McEnroe —acting again as an individual rather than as part of a corporate protest—fights on the spot. Thus attention for a widely held dissatisfaction with certain aspects of professional tennis and its management is focussed roundly on the most vociferous public complainer. McEnroe gets the wooden racket for drawing attention to the situation.

In 1981, during the Queens tournament, even the *Daily Telegraph* commented, 'There have been far too many late or changed calls, quite apart from the many disputed ones and the general standard has been well below that set by the Professional Tennis Umpires Association. One of McEnroe's complaints was that the umpire, despite a number of requests, did not turn off his microphone before speaking to the players and one had sympathy with the defending champion on this issue.' Since McEnroe had, during the course of this match, asked the umpire if he would care to jump in the lake and had charged him, after being warned for verbal obscenity himself, of 'obscene umpiring', one can begin to imagine the standard of officialdom. If the *Telegraph* could give a version of events that was sympathetic to McEnroe, it must have been quite low.

In 1979 and already tipped to topple Borg from the peak of the pro tennis mountain and already typecast as a bit of a hooligan, McEnroe nonetheless gave a good account of himself in the *News of the World*. He told his interviewer that although his earnings for the first six months of the year approached $800,000, he still appreciated life's little things. Like the ten dollar bill his grandparents had sent him for his birthday. 'They've sent me ten dollars a year since I was born and they did the same this year. I don't know if they're aware

128

of how much money I've made. All I know is they watch me on TV. But it's that kind of thing that keeps my feet on the ground.'

At that stage, before going into property and buying homes in Florida and Manhattan, all McEnroe could think of where spending sprees were concerned was cars (for his brother Mark as well as himself) and a good stereo.

'I'd rather be thought of as the bad boy of tennis than not to be noticed at all. But I figure people don't know me. They're judging a book by its cover and they don't understand. The trouble is I don't always know what's behind the cover myself. I know I'm shy. I know I always want to win. And that's about it. I may be quite famous now, but I'm still human. I have feelings. Of course I want people to like me. I think there are good things about me.'

'It's a bit of a jungle out there and you've got to learn pretty quick how to read people. All the things people say about me, all the names they call me, it only makes me more determined to win. Sure I do a bit of spitting on court, but I don't do it deliberately and I never do it on an undercover court.' I suppose that makes it okay, does it John? And as a matter of fact, if you don't do it on purpose how can you be sure you don't do it indoors? However, let that pass with a penalty point. 'It's just a nervous habit, but I reckon the day I don't will be the time to get out because then I won't care any more,' McEnroe said. 'Sometimes I wish I could just take a year off and go to Hawaii and lie in the sun. Sometimes Stacy and I just want to take off and go somewhere together. But you can't drop any job for six months and disappear, and tennis is my job.' McEnroe said that sometimes he did blow his top privately as well as on court but only with close and trusted friends. Of his court tantrums he said, 'I want to get to the point where when someone calls me an idiot I don't react. I don't answer back . . . I think the only thing that could really hurt me badly now would be if one of my close friends turned his back on me because of what I am and what I've become. I would find that really hard to handle. I'm not complaining about this fame thing but I find it hard to grasp when people call me a celebrity. I feel like a normal kid who plays tennis for a living and is good at his job.'

The professional code of conduct is, of course, partly devised to prevent and discourage tennis players from being beastly on court however badly they might feel like exploding angrily. At the moment abuse of ball or racket (slamming, kicking, beating the head on the court—that sort of thing), carries a fine of $300, and an obscene gesture rates $400. McEnroe has been fined more than any other player in the game's history—his Wimbledon 1981 fines were the highest ever levied. He doesn't have the franchise on bad calls—other players get them too—but most of his fellow pros find it easier to keep quiet.

'I don't care if I don't smile on court. That's me out there and people can take me how they like. When I get angry I could play better because of it,' McEnroe admitted. He considers that he's entitled to act more or less as he pleases on court and will say (sometimes) that crowds too are entitled to behave any way they want. On the other hand he's quick to show disdain and irritation when they make too much noise or heckle him.

The one thing on which he is consistent is officialdom, if he thinks it is sloppy or otherwise wanting. Understandably, perhaps, since the crowd's opinion as to whether a ball is good or bad is irrelevant while the umpire's decision is crucial. McEnroe's inconsistancies are many: needing or spurning popularity, grass or clay or concrete as his favourite surface, hating himself for getting angry or using it to fuel his game are just some of the mysteries. He's paradoxical, like all human beings. But unlike most humans, he's often quoted and things he may have said in irony, extremis or jest are immortalised in print. And thus are mythologies born.

Some people have had kind words for McEnroe. Billie Jean King, now very well-liked despite her cussingly controversial early years at Wimbledon, called Mac a genius when he was only nineteen. John, draping his arm round her shoulder, said then that his ambition was to do as she had, and win nineteen Wimbledon titles.

Tennis writers, while acknowledging that he has the potential to be as great a champion as Laver, Hoad, Borg, Gonzales or Budge, seem torn. Watching him, one wrote, was like having stereo earphones with Rachmaninov coming out of one side and Alf Garnett from the other. He makes such wonderful copy that the press would be impoverished without him, his antics or his tennis. If he is unpopular with the press and with the All England Club (whose membership, incidentally, represents about three millionths of the population of Britain) it should not be assumed that he is universally reviled. These people have the power to create images and sustain them. The question of McEnroe's post Wimbledon appeal against fines imposed there in 1981 (still unresolved at the end of the year)* rested, ironically with Harry Hopman, the Australian who coached the budding Wunderkind in the rudiments of the game at Port Washington. He was appointed as McEnroe's representative at his much-delayed final appeal to the Professional Council. Before the verdict was announced McEnroe was philosophical about it all. Sportsman-like, even. How would he react if he lost—not just the money, but the honour that was at stake? Having already suggested that the All England Club were pressurizing the council for a 'get McEnroe' verdict, having fought the case with passionate, apparently righteous fervour for many months, McEnroe simply said, 'Well I'd be disappointed, but I guess I'd just have to accept it.'

Certain factions agree that McEnroe has been the victim of almost vindictive line and chair decisions, that umpires can be almost insultingly authoritarian and that the stiff, correct and sometimes self-satisfied nature of officialdom makes a fiery cocktail when mixed with McEnroe's brand of intransigence and volatility. No-one's all right or all wrong but while it's certain that there's a trace of *pour encourager les autres* in decisions against McEnroe, his own drive is a combination towards winning and perfectionism. Ironically most of the trouble he gets into is because he wants things to be perfect.

On perfectionism he said, 'I don't really think I'm that close, but the idea of it motivates me. I'll never get there, but I'll improve.' Talking about his responsibilities to the game

*In January 1982, after a final hearing of his appeal against the fines, the case was resolved in McEnroe's favour over the fines quashed.

in late 1981 when he was ranked No. 1 in the world, he said, 'I would be happy with myself if I thought I'd given something back to the game. The rows rankle. I'll never forget Wimbledon and I've had the problems and pressures of a lifetime. But I think I'm calmer now. What I want to do is stay No. 1. for a while, to win the major tournaments. I'd just like to be respected for my game.'

Quietly, McEnroe has gone out of his way to spread his success around. As well as endowing Stanford with a lucrative tennis scholarship, he has given money to Trinity School to enable New York kids who would otherwise be unable to study there to get a first-rate education. He is generous with friends and protective and loyal to those he cares about. He told the *Daily Mail*, 'Sometimes it's nice to be able to pay and maybe if they feel uncomfortable I tell them to pay me back in five years when they're making it too.'

He even has a friend or two amongst Britain's pool of top-level officials. Ian Stirks, a 30 year-old from Barnstaple in Devon, was a linesman during the Benson and Hedges final in 1981 where amid stunning and rhapsodic tennis, McEnroe had a number of altercations, and ultimately lost to an equally belligerent Connors in five sets. 'Crowds upset McEnroe more than most players. He must have felt he was in a Roman ampitheatre. The crowd were out for blood and were not happy until they got it. As soon as McEnroe went to query a decision, which he was entitled to do, they wanted something to happen and they goaded him until it did. I umpired McEnroe in the doubles semi-finals the day before and he was well-behaved but the crowd was kinder, probably because in doubles they don't identify with one person so much. I thanked McEnroe after the match and I think he appreciated that.'

Years ago Roy Emerson asked why bad behaviour was afforded more publicity than good tennis. The obvious answer is that by its nature, news is the exceptional and by happy coincidence for newspaper sellers, any bad news about McEnroe—whose behaviour is exceptional by tennis standards, in every sense—will sell papers. Tennis has had ogres in the past. Connors, Gonzales and Nastase have all been

132

A rare smile from the 1981 Wimbledon champion.

(Daily Telegraph Colour Library)

seen as disruptive, rough-house boys and all have weathered it in the end. When a player reaches sporting maturity before intellectual maturity—think of those dancing fleas the eastern Europeans call gymnasts or the young swimmers who train for their Olympic golds before school every morning—the pressures of success are almost sure to provoke immature reactions and stressful outbursts. Sure, it's great to have unlimited pocket money when you're an eighteen year-old phenomenon and it would certainly be artificial to suggest that all that travel, prestige, excitement and glamour make for a miserable, tiresome, rotten life. But nonetheless all that has to be coped with by a young person who almost inevitably is simultaneously going through the routine adolescent problems and agonies.

One difference between McEnroe and the other tennis bad boys is that there is little flippant about his behaviour. 'I find it very hard to relax on court. I was brought up to be serious. If I joked around, did things that are pleasing to the crowd, maybe I wouldn't do as well.' No self-conscious, religiously anti-establishment rebel. Simply someone who is naturally prickly, intolerant and actually rather kind and generous as well as being intransigent and occasionally pompous. And someone who has a ghastly chemical reaction with Wimbledon which will almost certainly get him into more trouble this year. Red rags to bullishness.

The colourful characters that tennis has thrown up over recent years have probably helped to broaden the popularity of and interest in the game, and may be one reason why the slightly prim and proprietorial tennis establishment in Britain resents someone who demonstrates that the shape of tennis to come is not entirely within the power of the game's traditional guardians. The faintly pompous 'Britishness' that applauds understatement and generally tends to the view that if someone has to rant to attract attention they aren't worthy of it. Hence the respect afforded in England to the chap who can attract a taxi or bring a waiter without effort. This attitude tends to condemn McEnroe first and appreciate his tennis afterwards. It would be nice if McEnroe's good side could surface on court sometimes, but kindness, loyalty and so forth are not so easily transferred to the court. One day, perhaps, his enjoyment of the game will begin to show and might win half the battle for him.

Oddly enough, although he's been called ugly, coarse-featured and potato-faced, Mac has his admirers. Quite early in his professional career he was besieged by tennis groupies who were determined enough to track down his hotel and ring him in the middle of the night. McEnroe seemed entirely unflattered, merely irritated, by such attentions. It was, he said, 'a real pain'. Unlike Borg who never has to suffer these nocturnal intrusions since all his calls are put through Lennart Bergelin in the first place, McEnroe deflected the intrusions personally. At his matches there has been a contingent of squealing schoolgirls in support, attracted possibly by his rebel image as much as by his muscular thighs, scarlet headband and the quality of his serve.

'I don't understand these 13 or 14 year-old girls who chase round after players. American girls don't do it so maybe it's just the way you people are,' he told an English journalist after an early Wimbledon. Perhaps because Mac has had a steady girlfriend since his mid-teens and eccentric though it may be, is secure in that relationship, he is largely unmoved by the attention of the nymphets.

The gold chain with a 'J' suspended from it that he wears at all times was given to him by Stacy Margolin, a classic Californian blonde whose relationship with McEnroe has survived many a crisis and separation. He says he needs her because she understands him. Judging from some of the extraordinary thoughtless and simplistic things that have been said about him, it is not surprising that Mac values someone who actually does understand and accept him.

Understanding goes far deeper than tolerating creased jeans and socks that don't match, comfortable old leather jackets and idiosyncratic eating habits. A relationship where-in he can be himself—neither performing on court nor being typecast in newspapers—is precious indeed. To have weathered several years of gossip and scrutiny as well as the separations imposed by their careers, the relationship must be solidly rooted in basic liking and friendship. Neither likes to discuss it much. Mac has frequently had sharp words with journalists who have, in his view, pryed. There have, however, been several occasions when Stacy has felt bound to speak up in John's defence over some alleged misdemeanor. During Wimbledon in 1979, when McEnroe was dubbed the monster, she spoke out. 'Things have been blown up out of all proportion, and I feel John has been unfairly treated. John is probably a hopeless case with the British people. They will never like him. Sometimes I get embarrassed by the way he behaves on court and I tell him so, but he doesn't look for trouble.'

There have been rumours that the romance was on the rocks. Two years ago McEnroe was seen on several occasions squiring top American fashion model Cheryl Tiegs around some of Manhattan's plusher night-spots. Twelve years older than John, Ms. Tiegs clearly enjoys the company of tennis stars, since a previous boyfriend was Vitas Gerulaitis. However, her supposed mixed-doubles with John did not go to the full three sets, and despite periodic furores John and Stacy are still together. Quite why she left Wimbledon so soon before last year's final is not known. There may, for John, have been a small sense of the Do Not Foresake Me Oh My Darlings since Stacy left him, as Grace Kelly had left Gary Cooper in *High Noon* just before the final shoot up in Main Street.

Certainly McEnroe felt tetchy enough about the subject to inspire a violent row with pressmen when questioned about it, but the two of them met in Montreal soon afterwards and kissed and hugged affectionately at the airport. Stacy is the same age as McEnroe and has said that marriage, for the time being at least, is definitely out. McEnroe has been less emphatic. He's spoken of the difficulties that their separations impose but that marriage is a possibility for the future . . . but there's plenty of time. 'Stacy is the most reliable person in my life, except for my parents. But it's tough because we don't see each other that much. She understands all the pressures and why I'm the way I am. That kind of understanding is more important to me than constant companionship.'

During Wimbledon 1981 when the great fines drama was at its most furious, McEnroe's sex appeal appeared to escalate accordingly. He was supposed to be turning down scores of offers of noctural consolation. Stacy wasn't worried. 'He doesn't need groupies. I'm his only girl,' she said before she flew away. Offcourt, she said, McEnroe was gentle and attentive. He would be a tasty fish for a groupie to hook but stated that the other girls were wasting their time.

'We have to snatch whatever time we can together, but he needs someone who is playing tennis competitively like he is. Sometimes he might be at one end of the world and I might find myself at the other. Then our only link is the telephone.' She said that spectators seemed to look for the worst side in her boy's character, to bait him and to enjoy it when the fuse ignited. Stacy thinks that one day John's temper will cool but that it will take a big shock of some kind to effect the change. After the first disciplinary measures at Wimbledon last year she said, in an apparent state of high anxiety about her boyfriend, that the fines might do him good, adding, 'There's nothing I can do. There's nothing anyone can do . . .' She, like the psychologists, took the view that in early, easy matches McEnroe needed anger to charge himself up whereas in an exquisitely poised match like the one with Borg, it wasn't necessary. She also gave the stock, catch-all excuse. 'He's shy.'

When Stacy's not around and there are no other friends to go out to eat with or visit the movies, McEnroe tends to stay in his hotel room and watch television. He's rarely seen out discovating with Vitas or Ilie. 'You need time alone to think. It's not exactly fun to lie on some bed in your room and watch TV between practice and playing but that's the way I want it.' Hotel rooms stacked with dirty laundry, racket cases and a different view from the window every week can be very dispiriting places. McEnroe has said that he can take the life now but that he'd hate to think he'd still be travelling the pro circuit for another fifteen years. 'When you travel and you're in a place maybe twice a year, you don't get much chance to make friends. In a way the more you win the less chance you have to get to parties. When you're winning, it's tougher. The pressures are just incredible.'

There are times, however, when McEnroe can relax. At home in New York he stays in his Manhattan apartment or visits the family. If it's the right time of year he'll go to

Florida. Things aren't so terrible. At any rate the pressures haven't destroyed his sense of humour. While the fines drama raged on he had his hair cut and commented wryly that at least he didn't have to worry about whether the new crop was harming his image.

In spite of being labelled lumpy and unattractive, there have been several signs over the years that he could have a film career if he chose to. He had a small cameo part in the film *Players*, starring Ali MacGraw and Dean Paul Martin (son of Dean) made in 1978 and filmed partly at Wimbledon. The story told of an older woman's relationship with a young tennis star, and also featured Pancho Gonzales. There was also the possibility of him starring in a film about a tennis player turned rock star. McEnroe, after reading the script, said it would be perfect for him. 'Every kid wants to be a rock and roll star and I still do.' However, the project foundered. Then he was offered the leading role in a proposed film about an American strip cartoon character called Archie, who is all freckle-faced insolence. A deal might still be made and McEnroe has told friends that a film career appeals to him. He was reputedly offered £250,000 to take the part when negotiations began. Just before Christmas 1981 he had discussions in New York with Elton John about making a single for Elton's Rocket Records label.

In a forthcoming documentary about Italian opera star Luciano Pavarotti, there will be a glimpse of Mac on court with the singer, in a sequence demonstrating how Pavarotti likes to relax. Pavarotti is apparently a keen tennis player despite his twenty-stone frame. When asked about the singer's ability to keep pace with Mac on court, a spokesman said 'He'll be alright. He has big lungs.' Theoretically there's nothing to stop McEnroe mixing a career in acting, singing or driving around New York City in a yellow cab, come to that, but it is unlikely that he will cede time for a second career until he has peaked in tennis.

When relaxing McEnroe drives his Cadillac and listens to his awesome pile of rock cassettes—Springsteen, Meatloaf and other rorty stuff. He travels everywhere with a four-speaker, portable tape deck. He has also been known to go to the odd party and recently, not long after his haircut, he went to a charity disco in New York. At one point a glass of beer was tipped over his head by fellow tennis player Peter Rennart but instead of acting crossly McEnroe was helpless with laughter. He retaliated shortly afterwards by pouring champagne over another reveller. Such antics may be construed as showing his human side, but it's also arguable that these, finally, are the acts of true hooligans . . .

As Kay McEnroe testifies, he has never been tidy and hotel rooms where he has stayed, like tables where he has eaten, are usually strewn with post-Mac debris. He still sends his laundry home. It would, however, be disingenuous to suggest that off court he is a completely ordinary young man who sees his friends, has a steady girl, eats junk food and on the whole prefers pop music and a quiet life to social grooving. There is very little about anyone with that kind of talent or money that can truthfully be called ordinary. Money does mean something to Mac. He plays tennis for a living because he is wonderfully gifted and it is his good fortune that it is a career that pays enormously well. As he has said, he sure as hell isn't going to give any of his prize money back.

McEnroe's tennis success has brought him further rewards from advertising and endorsements. Every time he appears on court it is a shot in the arm for the Italian company who make his tennis clothes. Every time he aces, the directors of Dunlop may mentally bank the profits from another score of racket sales.

The Dunlop Maxply Fort is the same racket that Mac's hero, Rod Laver, used when he won the grand slam in 1968. Perhaps that is why McEnroe chose to use this 'off the peg' racket rather than a more common, modern graphite model. His racket is strung to 62 lbs.—slack compared to Borg's 86 lb. pressure. Until his grip changes his rackets will all be made at Horbury, near Wakefield in Yorkshire and they have served him well so far. Since he made the deal with Dunlop early in 1981 he has won Wimbledon, the US Open and a host of other titles. Dunlop will probably feel that his association with their product is well worth the price they paid to get him to endorse them. McEnroe gets through about forty rackets each year and will collect spares as he needs them from Dunlop agencies all over the world.

It would indeed be interesting to know if the sales of the Maxply Fort have soared since Mac signed his contract. Can people really be persuaded that they can raise their game by following the leader? It would also be interesting to know whether there is the faintest glimmer of cynicism on McEnroe's face when he reads the advertisements which quote him as saying, 'I wanted a wood racket and was determined to go out and look for the best.' However, everyone seems happy, and for this wealthy young man winning matches may be the most important thing, but money counts. Just a bit. When he first had success as a professional McEnroe used to advertise Seven Up, the fizzy rival to Coke. But as his happy-go-lucky kid image faded so did his face from the ads and the association ended. Teenage style fizz did not nestle happily with his new 'brat' image.

'I'm not concerned about the money. I figure as long as you keep winning the money's going to come in. I'm more concerned about the tennis,' he said. But even if Mac never wins another match he's probably got enough stashed away to keep him in fast motors, to enjoy the restaurants and night life of Manhattan, to live as well as he likes for the rest of his life. Perhaps when he has more time on his hands he'll turn more seriously to music. He can already play the guitar but has said he'd like to learn another instrument—probably the piano.

Some things don't change, though. Every year since 1978 McEnroe has said that he's a lot calmer and cooler than he was the previous year, that he can control himself now. Inch by inch it may be happening, but at Wimbledon especially it seems to be two steps forward and at least one step back. He'll probably still be saying he's more mellow now than last year in 1989.

A further word on the great McEnroe v Wimbledon debate from the New York based *Daily News*. 'Tennis is lucky to have a temperamental, salty-tongued Wimbledon champion such as John McEnroe and the tiresome little men who run the tennis championships will never understand what

Tennis elbow. McEnroe storms out of Heathrow in disgrace after winning the 1981 Wimbledon final.

(Photo: Paul Fievez/Associated Newspapers)

error they directed at McEnroe. That is how they can turn the world's greatest tournament into the worst!'

One of the 'tiresome little men', Sir Brian Burnett, was unable to comment at first, but Lady Burnett said, 'That's nice, isn't it?' Sir Brian later added, 'Absolute and utter rubbish! It's just laughable.'

9

THE PITS AND THE PENDULUM

It is anarchy in tennis shoes   *Peter Thomas, Daily Express*

I hate the umpires in this place*

I tell you, they were out to get him this year
 Ilie Nastase

His behaviour doesn't bother me. He's not malicious   *Stan Smith*

What I did was bad and wrong. Why do I do it?*

No-one, not even Borg, can go on winning at Wimbledon. His day has got to come and I intend to be there when it does*

Shut up*

The verbal exchanges added more spice in the second set. It was as if Kingsley Amis had written 'Lucky Jim' for Connors. McEnroe had thirteen break points in the second set—and still lost it   *Guardian*

A Wimbledon final isn't like anywhere else*

It is a pity McEnroe doesn't appreciate the difference between arguing his case and insulting people   *Ronald Atkin, Observer*

If McEnroe wants to win Wimbledon he should stop talking about the past. By re-hashing things he is just stoking the feud   *John Newcombe*

I'll just have to figure a way to beat him. That could take some time*

People are going to say what they want to say, write what they want to write . . . [the fines are] malarky*

We are talking about a minor unpleasantness . . . Wimbledon is just bombast. The impression is that they are out to get you   *John McEnroe Sr.*

It's a retrograde step for humanity   *Centre Court spectator*

They believe they are victims, father and son, paranoid about the place and pompous traditions which, it must be admitted, border on the preposterous   *Ken Jones, Sunday Mirror*

I want him to win because tennis needs him   *Pete Murray*

It stinks*

You're a disgrace to mankind*

You're an incompetent fool*

You're the pits of the world*

There are absolute insanities whenever you play him   *Sandy Mayer*

144

He's a swine in short *pants   American newspaper*

I don't care about the public's reaction as long
as I feel good about myself. The BBC reported
I'd got a speeding ticket . . . what gets me is
the lies. Newspapers write lies. Television reports lies*

John McEnroe

Few sportsmen can lay claim to having introduced a new
phrase into the English language. Muhammad Ali, maybe,
with 'Float like a butterfly, sting like a bee' and 'I am the
Greatest'. No individual footballer stands out among the
many who have been sick as parrots. Even Tony Grieg's
startling 'We'll make them grovel' of the devastatingly
successful West Indies touring side in 1976 passed out of the
language pretty sharpish. John McEnroe, however, may have
to win Wimbledon several more times before his lasting
cultural significance exceeds the durability of the phrase 'the
pits of the world.' Uttered on the Centre Court on the very
first day of Wimbledon 1981, McEnroe claims he was
addressing himself. Umpire Edward James thought otherwise.

Like many of McEnroe's ephithets the phrase is oddly,
polysyllabically clumsy. He seldom goes in for tart, brief
expletives. In any case, the pits of the world were spat out
during his opening match and soon shattered hopes of a new
superclean Superbrat. Maybe it reassured a few people who
thought things can be a little dull if McEnroe ain't misbehavin'.

Arriving in England for his usual warm-up at Queens
and the Stella Artois event, McEnroe had promised to be
good. Certainly a new leanness and even greater speed as
well as grace and elegance on court—helped to support the
fancy that some of the whelpish rancour had melted away

145

with the fat on his thighs. At eleven stone four now he was rangy for an athlete pushing six foot. Three months waiving of junk food had done the trick. He spoke on arrival with forthright intelligence, but with a mellow, analytic maturity too.

He had, he said, hated being at Wimbledon in the past but he now realised that the bad times had been mostly his own fault. He could forgive and forget now and wanted to start afresh with the people here. Whilst confirming that the title was his biggest ambition, he enumerated the ways he thought the championships could be improved. Better treatment and facilities for players, changes in some of the more pointless rituals and so forth. The scrappy moustache of 1980 had been shaved off. 'If I'd won that final match it would have stayed, but it wasn't coming through anyway. No-one knew what it was.' The red headband remained. He was, he said, finally free of the thigh, back and ankle injuries that had nagged on and off for four years but there were those who wondered if the new slim Mac, who hadn't been put through a five set match all year—still had the stamina to win. A panel comprising Lew Hoad, Fred Perry and Don Budge had no such doubts. They were ready to name McEnroe as the International Tennis Federation's player of the year.

Before Winbledon, traditionally, came the Stella Artois tournament at Queens Club. Here McEnroe's rest and renewed vigour was immediately obvious. He reached the final without dropping a set and a capacity crowd watched him pocket £8,500 after beating Brian Gottfried 7-6, 7-5 on one of that summer's few hot, bright days. The match took an hour and forty minutes and was closely fought with Gottfried having set point three times in the first and recovering again from set point at 4-5 in the second to have two set points of his own at 5-4 in the next game. The match was memorable both for fine serving from both men and for McEnroe's comments about the umpire, Mrs. Georgina Clark from Banbury. Displaying a sexism it is difficult to dismiss as simply another aspect of psyching-up, McEnroe told her that women shouldn't be allowed to officiate in major mens' matches. 'It's harder to get upset with a woman,' he said. Gottfried was more reasonable. 'Let her alone will you? An umpire is an umpire regardless of sex'. Later Gottfried asked McEnroe if he was having woman trouble. 'Me?', answered McEnroe, 'No, I've got a nice girlfriend.' After the match McEnroe said, 'I can see no reason why there should be a woman in the chair in a man's match. Men should deal with men.'

Mrs. Clark, accused by McEnroe of having ruined his match, was sanguine afterwards. 'I honestly didn't get angry with him. I am just sorry it made the news because I'd rather no-one noticed me.'

Despite Superdad's somewhat partial denial that tantrums were a tactic in his son's game ('there are certain things that are part of people's personalities' implied staunchly that stage-managed rows were not part of John's) there was deep cynicism about the 'reformed' McEnroe when Wimbledon opened.

Someone had a good word for him, though. 'He really is a pet,' said Judith Craig, the sculptress who had fashioned the wax model of McEnroe for Madame Tussauds. Borg's figure is there too, in the Heroes Room, but McEnroe's waxwork has yet to grace that particular court. Mac was stunned by the accuracy of the model although he added that it looked healthier than he did. Mr. Craig said that McEnroe had been most cooperative and patient during their sittings. 'I think he's charming', she said.

Borg came to Britain with the French Open title freshly won. He'd won the Masters early in the year and was set for the slam. Only one man, William Renshaw, has ever won Wimbledon six successive times and Bjorn wanted to emulate that English gentleman's 1881-1886 feat. A win in 1981 would also have equalled Roy Emerson's record of twelve grand prix titles in one year. Borg was on a hot streak and few of the tennis pundits could disguise the fact that they hoped he'd win this year. The last time someone whose initials were not B. B. had won Wimbledon had been when A. A. (Arthur Ashe) won in 1975. By the laws of philology it could just be Raul Ramirez's turn, or Stan Smith's .

The day of McEnroe's opening match was a scorcher, with McEnroe's temper rising with the temperature. He won 7-6, 7-5, 6-3 against Tom Gullikson but landed in trouble and disgrace which was to haunt him throughout the chamion-ships and afterwards. After declining several of McEnroe's requests to reverse line judgements, umpire Edward James was called 'the pits of the world'. When referee Fred Hoyles came out on court McEnroe called him 'an incompetent fool'. Next day the papers were referring to four letter words, although Mr. Hoyles admitted that the word used had not been a 'serious' one, so for a while many people may have thought that a far harsher insult than 'fool' had been applied.

'What I did was bad and wrong. Why do I do it? I only hurt myself,' said McEnroe, who was fined £750 for his words, afterwards. He seemed contrite, but it was too late. In the match he had twice been penalised a point. Another outburst would have lost him a game and disqualification would have come next. Mr. Hoyles warned McEnroe that further misconduct would be construed as 'aggravated behav-iour' and curiously phrased though the warning was, its message was loud and clear. McEnroe was pretty much assured of a hostile reception for the rest of the tournament.

Loyal as ever, Superdad backed John. 'On substance he was right, but on form it was not the way to act.' Too many line judges, he went on, took an active interest in the match instead of simply observing the placement of the ball.

The incident says much about McEnroe's court troubles. Any player is entitled to query any call that he is unhappy about. The fact is that most players seldom bother, partly because it is rare to get a decision reversed and partly because, at Wimbledon especially, it simply 'isn't done' to argue. Win some, lose some—it should even out, anyway, over the match. McEnroe queries calls because he appears to feel victimised by officials and rarely believes that over the course of a set or match that he will probably be the benificiary of an equal number of borderline calls. In contrast to the other chap's quieter approach, his behaviour seems the more vehement. He's probably right in thinking that a subtle, polite request will get him nowhere and since he may feel personally attacked by a dubious call he will fight back. In this incident, and others, he may have been penalised almost as much for venturing to complain as for the foolishly violent expression of his complaints. Maybe he should ask nicely first and then raise his voice. Maybe he should see it's better to button the lip altogether at times.

'Sometimes they get onto him for little things when other players get away with it,' said Stacy Margolin. 'When that happens he thinks everyone is out to get him and he starts yelling. But it doesn't pay to get mad. It doesn't pay to fight the system.' Meanwhile, on another court, Ilie Nastase was also being fined for bad language. *Plus ça change* . . .

So, with the threat of expulsion ringing in his ears, McEnroe moved into the second round of Wimbledon 1981. Rain was now making long work of some of the matches in the first week and a couple of days later his tussle with Ramirez was interrupted and finally stopped by bad weather. Watched by the Duchess of Kent, there was surprisingly warm applause for both men when they walked on court. McEnroe took the first set and had a fight on his hands at 5-5 in the second when the match was abandoned. Resumed the following day, it did not take McEnroe long to finish things off and push forward to the third round.

Three days after Wimbledon began an American radio station asked Mac how he'd felt over the past forty-eight hours.

'I was pretty down. Those things have got to affect you. But you try and roll with the punches. It's a lot harder that way, but I'm a fighter so I give it a try,' he told them.

Meanwhile, in a lull between his matches, 'Disgusted of Tunbridge Wells' and his cousins all over the country were dipping their pens in vitriol and the outraged letters which appeared in the newspaper columns towards the end of the week were roughly nine to one in favour of McEnroe being run out of the championships. Some merely suggested a damn good thrashing or a penalty set. One or two mildly suggested that maybe he wasn't as bad as all that, not really. Many of the letters could have taught McEnroe a thing or two about invective and spluttering rage. Journalists, too, were on the offensive.

'Had McEnroe reacted like that on a soccer field we would have screamed for his head, demanded he be banned for having brought the game into disrepute,' wrote Peter Thomas in the *Daily Express*. He then went on to more extreme themes. 'He will have established a standard of behaviour that will *naturally** be copied by every kid on every municipal tennis court in the country.' Advocating leadership and discipline Mr. Thomas went on: 'Once the authority of the umpires has been flouted, the next target is the policeman at the gate, then the copper on the beat. The young defy their parents and their teachers. It is infectious. An uneasy restless aggression that feeds on disobedience. It is anarchy in tennis shoes, suddenly walking the streets of life in bovver boots.' Good gracious, now there's a bit of lateral thinking.

Not all the newspaper criticism was quite as strident as Mr. Thomas's but much of it made the same points in milder words. Given all this I'm surprised that McEnroe was not held directly responsible, later on that summer, for the Brixton and Toxteth riots.

Into the third round and up against fellow American Bob Lutz. As if to remind McEnroe to watch his manners Fred Hoyles and his assistant Alan Mills put in a 'heavy mob' style appearance in the members' stand during the match, but there really wasn't any need. Mac was in spell-binding form and there was no nastiness. The opening set was fairly well balanced but with the advantage of the service break McEnroe really opened up his range and with breathtaking drop volleys and little dipping net skimmers he soon had things very much his own way. Meanwhile Borg had more trouble than he might have hoped for in dismissing Rolf Gehring of West Germany, who made him play very hard in the first two sets of their 6-4, 7-5, 6-0 match. Connors was troubled briefly in the first set of his match with Tony Giammalva but took it 6-4, 6-4, 6-0. Wet courts made for much slithering and slipping. Gerulaitis beat Victor Amaya and Stan Smith had a straight sets win over Balazs Taroczy of Hungary. This victory meant that Smith was the only seed left in Mac's side of the draw.

*My italics. 1A.

You'll go far, young man. Nancy Reagan with John McEnroe and Peter Fleming, September, 1981.

(Photo: David Hume Kennerly/TIME magazine)

When the rangy old warrior (all of thirty-three years old!) stepped onto the Centre Court to meet McEnroe in their fourth round match, there was little doubt that he was crowd favourite. His appearance has changed little with the years and he still looked the upstanding, soldierly gentleman he appeared when he won the magnificent 1972 final with Nastase. That match went to five sets and was played on Sunday because of foul weather on finals day. He's been a Wimbledon favourite ever since. Descibed by one journalist as 'a marvellous ambassador for the game which McEnroe hauls through the dirt', Smith himself was gracious as well as realistic about his young opponent. 'McEnroe's given me a lot of trouble. His behaviour doesn't bother me. In reality he's just a perfectionist who has a hard time holding his temper. But he's not malicious.'

McEnroe needed four sets to beat Smith and he seemed a little uneasy and caged on court. His 7-5, 3-6, 6-1, 6-2 win took him into the semi-final with the unseeded Johan Kriek from South Africa. The first two sets of the Smith match were evenly poised but as McEnroe settled into the match and his touch became surer there was no gainsaying the advantage of young legs over older ones. Smith could match neither speed nor service. In the first set, leading 5-4, there had been massive cheers for each of his points. Later, in the second set, McEnroe's concentration flagged and Smith's burst of winners caused huge excitement. McEnroe sulked a little and had relatively mild criticism for the line calls afterwards. He mumbled through the fourth set and there were a few 'Play on Mr. McEnroe's' from the chair. But Smith disputed a call, too. In that many points were closely fought and even towards the end of the match there were sharp net exchanges and Smith staged some short recoveries, it was an altogether absorbing contest. Apart from McEnroe, the remaining seven men in the championship were Kriek, Connors, Rod Frawley, Vijay Amitraj, Tim Mayotte, Peter McNamara and Bjorn Borg.

McEnroe's quarter final was an uncomplicated match. Except for some trouble in the third set where he seemed tense while Kriek extended himself with his strongest serves, McEnroe had few problems. Kriek did well to climb back from 0-4 down in the third, but after the tie-break McEnroe was very much in charge again.

In his semi-final match against the unfancied but vociferously welcomed Rod Frawley, from Australia, McEnroe's temper broke again. During the course of the match, which he won 7-6, 6-4, 7-5, he made a total of thirteen complaints. He was given a public warning by umpire Commander George Grime, whom McEnroe allegedly accused of being 'a disgrace to mankind'. Mac maintained he'd been castingating himself. Neither the umpire nor Fred Hoyles believed him and the cloven hoof earned McEnroe yet another penalty. The match lasted just over three hours and the fireworks began in the first set.

In the ninth game McEnroe disputed a line call on a ball which the umpire had confirmed as out. While he waited for Frawley's next serve he muttered 'I hate the umpires in this place.' He earned a warning for unsportsmanlike behaviour. The 'disgrace to mankind' controversy occurred in the third set and the point he had deducted then cost him a game to Frawley. He also addressed some hecklers in the crowd as 'vultures' and played magnificently in between fights.

'I'm not going to say they are gunning for me, but you can see by the way they act that they want to show their force. They look at me differently. They think I'm going to cause trouble. I can't breathe, hardly', said a somewhat paranoid McEnroe afterwards of the officials. During this press conference he also accused some journalists of kindling hostility and being liars. One member of the press asked him why Stacy had gone home and McEnroe replied angrily that it was no-one's damned business but his own. Another journalist took up the 'liars' theme and McEnroe railed on about the English press, encouraged by a contingent of American journalists. One English reporter admitted later that he was so incensed that he punched an American. More people joined in the fracas and as McEnroe left the conference, nine people were said to be on the floor!

The match with Frawley had been watched by Lady Diana Spencer but when the unpleasantness began she was discreetly ushered out for tea. Judging from her apparent delight at McEnroe's triumph in the final she might have preferred to stay and root for him.*

While the crowd were treated to a display of wit, wisdom and wizardry from McEnroe, another equally dramatic match took place on the Centre Court between Borg and Connors. In an intense and rugged match Connors astonished the crowd by grunting through the first two sets to take them 6-0, 6-4. Cheered though I was, to see Borg hitting some trouble; undeniably spirited though Connors performance was; I was glad when Borg roared back to take the next sets 6-3, 6-0, 6-4. It would have been an anti-climax if the ice and fire confrontation in the final was stymied. The Borg Connors match was a classic contrast of masterly control and whole-hearted, punishing strength. The result had much to do with Borg's relentless calm in the face of the early bombardment. A fine dress rehearsal for Saturday.

On Friday we all took a breather, except Chris Evert Lloyd and Hana Mandlikova who played tennis on the Centre Court (Mrs. Lloyd took away the big plate at the end) and John McEnroe and Peter Fleming who won the men's doubles.

*M*c*E*nroe on *B*org

Left-handers give him trouble

I have the perfect game to play him

My wide left serve will always worry a two-handed backhand player

*One Centre Court wag called, 'The wedding's off! Her ears are no longer virgin!'

You have to vary your pace

If I let up my concentration, even for a few seconds, the match is over

You must have patience

He's got a strong body and he can last indefinitely

He's faster than ever

You have to concentrate on every point or he'll pass you

His first serve is damned good

He's developed the second serve

Sure we act differently on court

Once in New Orleans when I went berserk over a bad call he gently waved his palms up and down to calm me down

When we play the match is always going to be interesting . . . with me rushing to the net and him staying backcourt

Sometimes when he and Connors play it's dull because they both play backcourt till someone misses

I want to beat him in Paris, on clay, over five sets

Left-handers give me trouble

If he serves badly his confidence drops quickly

He is incredibly fast

He is the master of the unexpected

To beat him I have to keep him pinned to the baseline by maintaining perfect length on my groundstrokes

I don't think he has the confidence to rally from the baseline

He could improve his groundstrokes

His serve is the best

Despite what you read, he's a nice guy*

When these two young men, Borg at twenty-four was two years older than McEnroe, walked onto the Centre Court on July 4th 1981 they were both playing for quite a lot more than the £21,600 that was at stake. For Borg there was the chance to equal the all-time record for consecutive Wimbledon wins, there were his hopes for that year's grand slam to sustain and there were the vast majority of spectators to please. For McEnroe there was a chance to prove that the fire and brimstone was part of a recipe for ultimate success. Maybe his habits would seem less than reprehensible if they could be shown to lead to undisputed mastery. There was the

* *Comments from Borg and McEnroe extracted from* BJORN BORG, MY LIFE AND GAME, *Sidgewick & Jackson, 1980.*

opportunity to beat Borg at the place it really mattered most. For both men there was also the chance to increase their street value as advertisers and endorsers. Everyone wants the Wimbledon champ to approve their wares. Dunlop admitted they expected a huge run on Maxply Forts if Mac won.

I wanted Mac to win, of course. Partly I wanted it this year because then no-one could say (as they might in two or five years time), that he beat Borg at Wimbledon when Bjorn was beginning to be past his best. 'You must develop a maniacal desire to win. For me that means expressing it in everything I do,' said John McEnroe.

'The madder John gets, the more Bjorn will like it,' said Arthur Ashe.

It was a fine, sunny afternoon, just like 1980, except maybe a little warmer. Bjorn and John hit a few to each other. Everyone knew that apart from the fact that they both wear headbands and play tennis that they didn't have all that much in common. In every sense this was going to be some kind of deep contrast not merely a match. No sense of grudge or animosity, but even more than in 1980 there was a sense of rooting violently for one man or the other. In the preceding twelve months Mac's copy book had become even more severely splodged and blotted. Borg's image, partly by virtue of his marriage to Marianna and his tenure at the top having been sustained for another year, was Mr. Cleaner Than Ever. King of the Heap and King of the Heat. Almost mythic, now, in his Norse mastery. More than ever they evoked stark opposites.

'No-one, not even Borg, can go on winning Wimbledon forever. His day has got to come and I intend to be there when it does.' How long ago had Mac said that? How long did he think it would take him when, four years earlier he'd got within one match of having his first tilt. The fourth of July. American Independence Day. John McEnroe's day.

The match, it must be said, was not quite the 1980's titanic battle. But it was tense and scorching none the less. From the moment that umpire Bob Jenkins (for once not an old soldier or retired wing commander but a traffic controller, appropriately enough) said 'Quiet please,' the Centre Court was hushed. The first McEnroe service uncoiled and the match was on.

In this first set McEnroe's service was so accurate and Borg's so shakey that McEnroe only needed to break serve once to take the set. But extraordinarily, he who was serving so much better, whose first serves were so often winners whilst Borg was playing a less aggressive game, was the one who was broken and in thirty-six minutes the set was over. McEnroe had saved four break points but Borg kept him away from the net and was always in the right place for the return. Borg took the set 6-4.

The second set opened with McEnroe's service and now he bit his lip when a serve that looked good was called out. This control was one of the key notes of the match for there was only one mild display of temper and only one or two scowls and truculent glances for the duration. Double faulting more than Borg but getting in more aces, the pattern of the match was established. Long, nerve-jangling rallies where Borg had the final edge and collected the point at the end swung to equally long passages when McEnroe's sure-footed speed took him to the right place at the right moment to play an unreturnable shot. Borg's backhand and groundstrokes were the best but his serve kept letting him down.

John was getting too many points in Borg's service games even if the Swede won the crucial last point. McEnroe had two break points in the second game but both were saved. There was a line call that McEnroe looked unhappy about, Borg took the game and McEnroe kept his cool. It was remorseless rather than blisteringly brilliant tennis and almost from the start of the set a tie break seemed inevitable. I was so tense and nervous I had to leave the room and place myself out of clear earshot of the television, but with the door open just wide enough to hear the great roar that went up when the tie-break was over. I had a little bet with myself that it would be two sets up to Borg when I returned. But after several minutes, a few false alarms and much loud cheering, the final howl went up. I found I owed myself money. John had evened the match by taking the set 7-6.

In the third set Borg began to look even more dangerous. Things began, and continued to go, badly for Mac. Borg

(A) Council of war. McEnroe and Connors, Wembley finals of the Benson & Hedges tennis tournament, November 1981.

(Syndication Int.)

(B) Shouting at the umpire.

(Associated Newspapers)

served first and held serve easily. McEnroe just held onto his own and next Borg did. Then he broke McEnroe's serve after Mac had lost game point with a double fault.

Borg held his own serve and went 4-1 up. Then Mac held his serve and the score crept back to 4-3. In the eighth game McEnroe had a lucky net call and then, on game point, sliced a low bounce which Borg could not possibly reach. It was 4-4. Borg held serve and then in the tenth game McEnroe played nervelessly to save three set points, bringing out the first service which had proved unanswerable before, producing volleys of searing beauty. At 6-6 it was time for a break.

Maybe McEnroe had time for a bite of a chocolate Kit-Kat at the changeover. In any case, he was in full command of the tie-break and won it surely seven points to four. Not like the 1980 marathon but good enough to give him a 2-1 set lead.

Borg opened the fourth on his own service—a strong advantage in his bid to level the match. But he looked tired and although games went with service it was always Mac who looked stronger. He didn't look happy, or relaxed, or cocky. He looked fraught and tense and worried but he looked fiercer. Borg looked weary and as if his legs ached. In the ninth game McEnroe broke serve and it was 5-4 to the American. For the first time since 1976 Borg was facing serve to stay champion. And what a serve. Still without looking happy or acting like he was moving in for the kill, a grim-faced McEnroe served for the match. It was a shorter game than many. With a slamming forehand volley to a part of the court that even Borg could not reach, McEnroe had won. Bye-bye, BB.

There was uproar, of course. Sadness for Borg, slumped on the turf that he had grown accustomed to kissing briefly at moments like this. Wild applause from McEnroe supporters and solid, generous applause from the others. It had been a great match and the better man had won. The cheers were for a great champion's Wimbledon defeat, for a new champion's impeccable tennis and for a thrilling match. I felt exalted and exhausted. Lady Diana (who'd clearly been rooting for Mac as every glimpse of her, every smile and reaction that the television had picked up, had shown), clasped her hands in pleasure. The cheers went on for minutes. In fourteen Borg-McEnroe matches the score was now even at seven all.

When McEnroe eventually collected the cup, a rather odd smile flickered across his face for a few moments. Just for once he looked pleased. I don't know how long it lasted. The announcement of his fines—at the time Wimbledon was suggesting a total of about £7,000 although this figure was later halved—came hot on the blistered heels of his triumph.

Every title changed hands at this particular Wimbledon and each one, except for the mixed doubles won by Betty Stove and Frew McMillan, went to Americans.

The big match had lasted three hours and twenty-two minutes. If you'd been rooting for McEnroe you'd remember it as a great match. Many of the tennis writers described it as exciting and dramatic but not as good, for example, as Borg's semi-final with Connors. Again it almost seemed as if they were trying to detract from McEnroe's victory by implying he beat Borg on a bad day. That the match was not quite first rate and that McEnroe was thus not quite proved as a first-rate champion. McEnroe, they said, had been lucky. He got nine out of ten first serves in during the tie-breaks. Luck has little to do with a performance like that under stress. Borg's anticipation, passing shots and raking backhands had all been stunning and it's a shame Mac's victory was not more roundly acknowledged. Borg had played very well, but only as well as McEnroe had allowed him, that day, to play.

One week later McEnroe played his next competitive match. It was tight and tense and he lost 4-6, 12-14, 5-7 to Ivan Lendl in a Davis Cup quarter final match at Flushing Meadow. Maybe he was tired, maybe the strain of the post-Wimbledon furore upset him, maybe any match, so soon after the Wimbledon final, was an anti-climax. In any case, Mac seemed dejected and, despite the standing ovation he got when he walked on court, unhappy and fractious. He's a funny one: says he hates playing in the cold, but maybe at 100 degrees it was too hot even for him. This time he was cheered and lionised. There was no wind or damp and he got off to a good start, but it wasn't his match. He played as well as Lendl—then No. 4 in the world—allowed him to play.

10

A FINE MADNESS

I am still the champion and they can't take that
away from me*

This year however the committee have decided
not to elect John McEnroe a member at the present time . . .   *All England Lawn Tennis and
Croquet Club*

If you profane Wimbledon it is like profaning
the Queen   *Arthur Ashe*

The crowd were out for his blood and were not
happy till they got it   *Ian Stirk, linesman*

You don't want robots on court*

Connors committed the same racket-throwing
and ball-slashing acts but it went unpunished by
the referee   *Laurie Pignon, Daily Mail*

I don't see how anyone can come on in Britain.
You have just as many players but you just
don't give them anything. No chance, no help*

The All England Club may think themselves important, but that opinion is not unanimously shared by outsiders *Rex Bellamy, The Times*

I feel sorry for John. The Wimbledon authorities feel they have almost divine rights *Jimmy Connors*

You cannot expect to become a member of a club whose traditions you have flouted . . . whose attitude you have affronted by your loutish behaviour and obscene language *Peter Wilson, Daily Mirror*

He called me a four-letter-word. It was not a very serious one *Fred Hoyles*

I always dreamed when I was a kid of being champion of Wimbledon and now that I am it's just great. That is the most important thing*

There's going to come a time when I won't let this sort of thing bother me*

John has got away with murder on court—and it has got to stop *Arthur Ashe*

McEnroe is dreadful and should have been kicked out after the first round *Jonah Barrington*

Some of you write a lot of lies*

I am sorry he is not here and as an American I apologise to you *Chris Evert Lloyd*

It was a classic example of over-reaction by authority *John McEnroe Sr.*

I shall pay for this tomorrow*

Fines don't matter to us *Jimmy Connors*

I've had better days *John Parry*

* *John McEnroe*

163

The big question remains unanswered. When John McEnroe stepped off Concorde back home in New York after the great Wimbledon Waltz furore, did he head off to see Springsteen or the Allman Brothers? Someone who had the pleasurable surprise of standing next to Mac during one of Bruce Springsteen's London concerts that summer said that McEnroe had his thumbs thrust through the belt loops of his jeans and bopped, or played imaginary guitar throughout. However the Springsteen theory is born out neither by Bruce's playing schedule or reports that it was the Allman Bros whom Mac went to see. He obviously needed something to take his mind off the fact that, on arriving time, he found that he really had been given the tennis elbow. He was not to be invited to become an honorary member of the All England Club.

'Am I going to be the first champion in 100 years to be excluded from automatic membership? I don't believe it's possible,' he said when he heard the news. Maybe he just went straight over to Douglastown for a long draw of fond, friendly air and restorative care.

McEnroe left England a champion without honour. After a dash to Concorde at Heathrow, punctuated by the sound of breaking glasses and china and the panting of journalists in disarray and pursuit the day after the final, he said of his non-appearance at the post-championship banquet, 'I didn't go because nobody asked me. They don't want me and, you know, it was fine with me.'

No-one could dispute his right to the title but he was robbed of—or threw away—just about everything else that becoming men's singles champion can offer. Even the prize money, which in McEnroe's case, as singles and doubles champion, was over £26,000 was slashed. In all McEnroe had accumulated fines of around £7,000, most of this collected as the price of temper outbursts during his semifinal match. He also risked suspension from the game for up to a year. The manner of the announcement of the punishments—just hours after his win over Borg, probably contributed heavily to the most controversial aspect of his post-tournament behaviour and the act that was deemed the most unforgivable of all by the tennis establishment. He failed to attend the banquet given by the All England Club at the Savoy Hotel in London.

McEnroe had stated before the event that he would not be able to spend the entire evening at the dinner, preferring to dine on pizza with friends and family in a restaurant. He said he'd like to arrive in time for the speeches and presentations and bring seven guests. The All England Club was unhappy with this request—they felt five tickets was a large enough allocation and in any case, they expect their star guests to be present for the duration of the evening. Mac said he'd be able to arrive by eleven. The All England Club compromised at 10.15 pm. There was deadlock and McEnroe did not show up. The club has denied that they point blank refused to accommodate McEnroe and his entourage and emphatically dismissed McEnroe's allegations that officials were 'obnoxious' to his father who'd been trying to negotiate an acceptable compromise.

Arthur Ashe understands that to profane Wimbledon is almost blasphemous in Britain. McEnroe may have found that if he had gritted his teeth and attended the banquet the All England Club might not have been quite so vigorous in their agitation for the fines and 'criminal record' to stick. Philippe Chartrier, chairman of the Professional Council that has been considering McEnroe's appeals has said, 'We will have to consider everything very carefully. We must not appear vindictive but we have to protect the game. It could be a long time before this whole business is settled.'*

After the first thunderclouds of the row had settled (but before the fines issue had been resolved) McEnroe spoke of events. He had a catalogue of complaints about the dinner furore and Wimbledon in general. Wimbledon, said McEnroe, was not about going to dances or anything like that. It was about winning. A congratulatory telegram from President Reagan, despatched immediately after he had won, had taken three weeks to be forwarded to McEnroe. It had bordered on the sadistic to sour his moment of greatest glory with news of the fines so soon after the match and to deliver

*It took six months.

165

the news just before the banquet. Surely they could have waited until the following day, or the Monday, since the fines, in any case, would hardly have been paid up without murmur on the spot. McEnroe found it unfair and distressing to be denied membership of the club, although officialdom's answer to this is pretty confounding. How could they grant honorary membership to someone they were simultaneously charging with bringing the game into disrepute? McEnroe is clearly not as much worried by the money involved as by the principle at stake.

He and his father contested the charges vigorously. Much of their defence rested on their emphatic claim that McEnroe's worst insults were self-directed, that it is no crime to talk to yourself. The club extended a bland olive branch when it expressed the hope that Mac would return to play in 1982 and that exclusion from the club was not finite —simply 'at the present time'. But even if McEnroe's play and manners are exemplary enough to take him to the title and honorary membership this year, it will take some time for him to forgive the rancour, accusations and, as he sees it, victimisation that led to counter-attack and mutual rejection in 1981.

Ashe has said that McEnroe must remember that the provocation he sees is often confined to his own imagination. Veteran American tennis star Gardner Mulloy saw McEnroe's behaviour as 'unforgivable,' and Mac might remember that previous champions like Fred Perry, Hoad and Laver had their membership withdrawn when they turned pro but were subsequently forgiven and reinstated. Ashe tried to calm Mac down, but Superdad said of the accusations, 'It is absurd. They can't make it stick. The courts were wired for sound and picked up those asides he was making to himself.' So the fight went on.

A couple of months after the debacle McEnroe spoke to Rex Bellamy in *The Times*. 'A guy showed me a picture taken when I'd won, and was on my knees. When I saw it I just thought how tough a time it was over there. Not the tennis, but everything else. But if you have any brains in your head going through a bad experience helps you. It has helped my attitude already. It's a little more enjoyable to play now. I feel more at ease.' This last a little premature,

Wembley, November 1981.

(Photo: Tony Duffy/Allsport Photographic)

perhaps. The high tension he'd shown, he said, was partly a result of basic distaste for the mannered gentility and seemingly pointless rules at Wimbledon and he claimed that other players, used to the more informal ambiance of lesser tournaments, found this hard to adjust to as well.

'It's really important to get over that hill at Wimbledon. Everyone was telling me I should win but at the back of my head was the thought that 'Nasty' and Rosewall had never won it. When it's taken for granted that you'll get to the final or the semis, you get nervous and uptight. That was definitely the reason I got upset in the first round.' He went on to explain how being a New Yorker influenced him. New Yorkers, he said, fought for what they thought was right. Direct confrontation. 'I've never tolerated phoniness in anyone and there's a lot of it at Wimbledon.'

He hastened to add that he was not generalising about England and that he enjoys playing at Wembley and Queens. 'It's just Wimbledon. It seems we're at opposite extremes —that everything I do is wrong to them and everything they did was wrong for me.' The no play on Sunday rule irritated him, he said, but what seemed more hypocritical was the rumour that this might now be changed if it brought enough money to the club.

McEnroe reiterated that he'd been willing to go to the dinner and had not deliberately snubbed it. Rather he felt that the rudeness to his father and the announcement of the fines had angered him. Honorary membership has been denied to few who genuinely deserve it. Angela Buxton, twice a ladies singles finalist and someone who has since given years of untiring service to the game, has been waiting for twenty years. Sir John Junor, in the *Sunday Express*, reported that she believes that she has been excluded because she is Jewish. Air Chief Marshall Sir Brian Burnett, Chairman of the Championship Committee, denied that McEnroe's exclusion was connected with his failure to attend the dinner. 'We couldn't on the one hand recommend that the Men's international Council should fine him for bringing the game into disrepute and on the other recommend him for honorary membership,' he said simply. So much happened in the day or two after McEnroe's win that it is difficult to perceive a precise sequence of events, let alone cause and effect. Almost certainly emotional responses affected the timing of events on both sides and it all left a nasty taste in McEnroe's mouth and a deep mutual suspicion. The establishment will make Mac work very hard to win a better image. In any case, ladies champion Chris Evert Lloyd coyly tried to fill in for Mac at the dinner. At speech time she remarked that she ought to make John's for him—but that she couldn't do so as she didn't have his vocabulary.

McEnroe and his father went on and on fighting the fines through many tribunals and hearings. By the end of 1981 things were still unresolved. Back home in the States there was little media support. Most pundits felt Mac deserved all he got. Often McEnroe has played at home to the likes of Borg with the crowd firmly on the other man's side. 'He's a swine in short pants', 'What does this disgraceful jerk have to do to be suspended for six months?', 'McEnroe has not only degenerated the game of tennis, he has betrayed his country', were typical comments.

McEnroe may have something approaching a persecution complex. 'The umpires are out to get me', and, of the press, 'It doesn't matter what I say, they'll write what they want anyway', are typical of him. As a result of feeling particularly hounded and misunderstood after Wimbledon he retreated further than ever behind the tough, scaly outer skin. One of the few people who had a good word for him then was Ilie Nastase. 'Not everyone should be like McEnroe but not everyone should be like Borg either. All McEnroe does is complain. Does he kill anyone? What does he do that is so horrible? I tell you, they were out to get him this year.'

McEnroe was reputed to have been willing to fly back to England to make peace but that the All England Club had declined this offer. It is a pity, if this is true. By November hostilities had again become so heated that Mac was accusing the club of threatening to withdraw from the Volvo Grand Prix circuit unless McEnroe's appeal to the professional council was blocked. This was, of course, denied. By September the club had halved their original fine for McEnroe's 'aggravated behaviour' but things still went to an independent appeal. McEnroe still strenuously denying all charges and the club denying accusations of pressurising. There will be deadlock until McEnroe pays up or the charges are withdrawn, or dismissed.*

Maybe Mac did call Fred Hoyles 'an incompetent fool' (after feeling that he had been wrongly accused of insulting the umpire) perhaps the other charges are valid. The sooner it is all consigned to history the better. At least he staved off suspension after Wimbledon and had the satisfaction soon afterwards of playing in the Davis Cup and then the US Open. It is also to be hoped that McEnroe's punishment, if any, is confined to breaches of discipline on court and not muddled with alarmist generalities.* Many were the remarks at the time that soon tennis crowds would behave like football hooligans and implied in these statements was the idea that it would all be Mac's fault if they did. Tennis crowds have their own style of genteel poor manners and really, doesn't it rather over-estimate even McEnroe's influence to suggest that he could turn masses of schoolgirls and matrons into a hurly burly of flick-knife bearing, tatooed, bother-booted delinquents ready to slash railway carriages' upholstery at the drop of an aitch?

On hearing the news of his barring from the club, back in New York, McEnroe said, 'I am still the champion. They can't take that away from me.' Jimmy Connors, a member since his singles final win in 1974 but unpopular with the establishment when he snubbed the Centenary Wimbledon champions' parade in 1977, commented, 'I feel sorry for John. The Wimbledon authorities feel they have almost divine rights.'

The statement that caused all the fuss read: 'This year the committee have decided not to elect John McEnroe a member at the present time in view of his behaviour on court in certain matches which, in their opinion, brought the game into disrepute.'

'He must realise that Wimbledon to the British is not just a tennis tournament. It is an institution. If you profane

*In January 1982, after a final hearing of his appeal against the fines, the case was resolved in McEnroe's favour and the fines quashed.

Wimbledon it is like profaning the Queen. I have given him a lecture,' said Arthur Ashe. This was rather more cogent than the barb from Lew Hoad who called McEnroe spoilt and childish and who, like Jonah Barrington, posited the view that being kicked out after the first round might have been the answer. This could be true: there would have been no unclaimed and lonely golden cup at the Savoy if Mac had been so disciplined. The great trophy would probably have been on its way back to Stockholm.

Last word on the issue from McEnroe. When asked by journalists if he intended to come back this year to defend the title he answered quickly. 'Would you ask any other champion that?' Oh no John. That, surely, is the whole, infuriating, glorious point.

After Wimbledon McEnroe had a fairly loose schedule for a few weeks. Enough tennis to keep in shape but not enough to stay under public scrutiny. He spent a lot of time at home watching videos of the final. He needed a rest but asked whether in view of the furore Wimbledon had been worthwhile, if the championship really was worth all the bother, he replied, 'Definitely.'

Despite playing to a home crowd at Flushing Meadow McEnroe was by no means popular favourite for the U S Open. Connors was the man most Americans wanted to win. At home, in matches from Dallas to New York Mac is booed and castigated and when he met Borg in the final of the Open most of the spectators were rooting for the blond bombshell. It's far too early to talk of Borg's retirement but it seemed in the 1981 Open final that some were watching it as if it were Borg's last great effort to take this elusive title—at his tenth attempt.

The match was a fairly interesting if fainter xerox of the Wimbledon final with Borg going down 4-6, 6-2, 6-4, 6-3 to McEnroe. By common consent it was not a patch on the earlier final. However, McEnroe became the first man since Connors in 1974 to win both titles in the same year. McEnroe accepts that on slower surfaces, especially European, Borg will often have his measure, 'but I am comfortable playing him on any other surface.' A change of attitude towards Borg is discernible here. No longer is McEnroe the kid who has

171

some lucky wins. He clearly sees himself as having earned a place among the top two or three. No trace of modesty and none of false humility either, not of chest-beating boastfulness. Just a realistic recognition of the facts: he now has Borg's number. He has proved it several times now, and in September 1981 he won the U S Open for the third successive time. Borg has been runner-up four times: this unfortunate record comes second only to Billy Johnson who had the bad luck to lose the U S Open final six times, mainly to Bill Tilden.

Borg was certainly under stress in the 1981 final. There had been a threat on his life before his semi-final. Opponent Connors was not suspected. Despite this tension he played a majestic match but a further threat was made before the final and a special police squad led him on and off court. This probably explains his non-appearance at the awards ceremony afterwards (a *much* better excuse than McEnroe's at Wimbledon) and he drove quietly away minutes after Mac had finished the match on his serve.

Afterwards McEnroe said he'd come into real form after the first set, when Borg had called all the shots. Bjorn threw away a strong chance to recover at 4-2 in the third set, but Mac's reply of five winning games on the run effectively determined the end result. Moments of brilliance, scintillating backhands and spinning lobs gave the game life again in the fourth set, but now McEnroe was seldom under real pressure. 'I couldn't really have asked for a better game. Suddenly I felt like I could hit any shot.' He said that being seeded No. 1 puts a special pressure on and he didn't like it much.

'It's a lot harder to stay at the top than to get there and I think Borg has been feeling the pressure somewhat in the last two years.' It was a match without pauses for argument. 'I did try to stay out of it. I've been involved with enough for a lifetime,' said the champ.

Later that autumn McEnroe played in Tokyo in the World Super Tennis Tournament. It's odd how each of the venues on the circus trail invents a name for itself, which implies it is terrifically important, while the one which by common consent really is the most prestigious simply calls

The duellist, Benson & Hedges finals against Connors, Wembley, 1981.

(Photo: Eamonn McCabe/The Observer)

itself the Lawn Tennis Championships. Top-seeded, McEnroe did not have the happiest of tournaments and there was even speculation that he would not return to England to defend his Benson and Hedges title. In Tokyo he was unexpectedly defeated by Vincent Van Patten in the semi-finals, 6-2, 3-6, 6-3. Including doubles, he'd played a total of thirteen matches in Japan. A disconsolate McEnroe was said to be reviewing his plans afterwards. He was, Van Patten said, 'grumpy and short-tempered', and he'd accumulated fines of $750 in both his second and third round matches. Not counting the Wimbledon fines which were 'on ice' he was now only $500 away from total fines for the year of $5,000 in a year, which would lead to a suspension.

Physically and mentally exhausted after the big tournaments and the Davis Cup, McEnroe was cramped in his tennis and nearing the end of his short fuse. Van Patten, named 'newcomer of the year' in 1979 by fellow professionals, announced after his stunning win that there was 'magic in the air.' Spoken, Vince, like the acting prodigy you once were. The magic has yet to work any further tricks or legerdemain. Vince Van Patten has since slipped back to a world-ranking in the eighties, but at least he had his moment.

So McEnroe came to Wembley in November to defend his Benson and Hedges title without the gloss and oomph of recent triumphs to inspire him. He came scared, probably, and wary of the kind of reception that marked his last visit and departure from Britain. He came to defend not only a title but a reputation and an image. He came with a threat of suspension and an unfriendly public to appease. He came not only with a chip on his shoulder, but the whole British fry-up, baked beans, sausages, fried bread and egg on his face.

It can only be conjectured. Just four months after one of the most scandalous departures from our shores since Oscar Wilde ran away to France, what exactly was going through John McEnroe's mind as he arrived at Heathrow in November 1981? On the one hand he was determined to be a good boy, on the other he was defensive. 'Change my image? Why should I? I have a great image.' As he was whisked through the VIP lounge his mood seemed to change every few seconds. Dressed in sneakers, jeans and with hands thrust deep into the pockets of the familiar battered bomber jacket he said, 'I don't know if I can get through a week in England with a clean slate. We'll just have to see.' Moments later flashes of the old defiance were showing. 'People said I wouldn't dare to return to England after last summer, but here I am.'

He'd come to defend his title for the third time. The Benson and Hedges tournament has a £95,000 total purse, but there were the final stages of the Wimbledon appeal hanging over his closely cropped head. For a few dollars more he could be suspended. Against all his instincts, perhaps, it was in his interest to behave in a studiously correct way. Some thought that this itself would be harder than winning any of the matches and I daresay he thought so too.

Whatever his reasons McEnroe arrived with some of the contrition of a prodigal. He behaved, so far as it is possible for a forceful personality to do so, with composure and dignity when he arrived. His first match was with the unfancied (excluding schoolgirls, optimists and immediate family) John Feaver, a British Davis Cup player who'd gained a place in the tournament through a 'wild card'. In other words, world ranking and logical 'earning' of a place to play was waived. 'Just my luck,' said the sporting Feaver of his draw. Up till now McEnroe, making his fourth appearance at the B&H event, had dropped only one set in fifteen matches. He and Fleming had also won the doubles three times in succession. Of the thirty-two players in the singles, nineteen were American.

Since 1934, when the first professional exhibition tournament was played at Wembley (and when Bill Tilden and Elizabeth Vines were dubbed as outlaws for robbing the deserving amateur poor of the prizes they morally if not technically deserved), this has been a venue for some of the best displays of tennis in Britain. Emerson, Laver, Newcombe, Smith and Nastase have all played at Wembley in recent years, thus lending it the status of an almost pukka amateur tournament. It was important for a number of reasons, very important for McEnroe to acquit himself well there. There might even have been the barest chance that his case against the Wimbledon fines could be helped if he showed himself as reformed and well-mannered.

After Peter Fleming was quickly dispensed with in the singles by British Jonathan Smith (another wild card player who took three hours over his 6-7, 7-6, 6-4 win), McEnroe's singles match was delayed because of doubles commitments. But he demolished Feaver quickly and went comfortably through to the semis where he met Sandy Mayer. His play was as relentless as the 6-3, 6-3 scoreline suggests. It took only 71 minutes, and with a single break of service in each set, McEnroe (snarling occasionally), was on top form.

Afterwards Mayer conceded that McEnroe had played 'phenomenally well' but said, of Mac's altercations with linesmen and judges, that McEnroe's conviction that he was always right was 'straight out of Camelot'. There had been needle in this match and McEnroe came perilously close to fines that could have stymied his progress. He ordered a spectator to sit down, queried one of Mayer's serves ('I have been known to hit a decent serve once in a while,' replied Mayer testily) and picked up a public warning from the umpire. The match, however, was not really worth the McEnroe angst (perhaps supporting the 'hysterical extrovert' view) and after a slightly shakey start he conceded only another twelve points to take the match.

Connors played the Frenchman Yannick Noah in his semi-final and won 6-3, 6-3. But judging from McEnroe's form, most people—even his worst enemies—would have put their money on McEnroe sweeping Connors off the court in the final.

'Abuse of ball or racket' in other words the slamming of one or the throwing of the other, each carries a $300 penalty. An obscene gesture carries a fine of $400. McEnroe had scant margin for error when he faced Connors in the final. Perhaps he should have placed a large piece of elastoplast over his mouth, just to be on the safe side, and to confine harsher thoughts to his own mind.

The final proved to be far more controversial than the Wimbledon climax. Played in a grudging atmosphere of latent fury and with a number of contested line calls and considerable audience participation, it brought out the very worst in McEnroe, and indeed in Connors. Mac took the first two sets in seemingly effortless fashion, 6-3, 6-2. Little applause came back from a packed Wembley and his face seldom cracked from the dour mask of concentration and familiar determination. Two sets up and apparently firmly in charge, his emotional stamina snapped during the third.

After dominating play, almost seeming to feed Connors the perfectly pitched shots which would ultimately win him the next point, an early indication of the simmering tension showed when after some cross talk over the net McEnroe was warned for misconduct and penalised a point. One wondered why Connors was not similarly warned since he'd taken part in the argument. Not apparently too ruffled by this argy bargy McEnroe had gone on to win the second set with near contemptuous ease, but he had been cast as bogey man and his concentration and confidence were seriously eroded.

This match was always going to be a prize fight but it had begun quietly. Using his huge range and giving Connors little room to employ his more limited armoury, McEnroe was cruising through and serving particularly well. His control, however, seemed studied rather than natural. It was a stupendous battle, marked by the quality and length of its rallies, but things began to go badly wrong for Mac in the third set.

Now the distinct characteristics of both these magnificent players were demonstrated to the point of embarrassment. Whilst McEnroe fumed, argued, stomped and thrashed his racket in despair, Connors swore, cussed and played to the gallery. In some ways Connors' behaviour, and his exploitation of McEnroe's psychological disadvantages were the most unsavoury aspects of the entire match. Knowing that most of the 9,000 assembled were rooting for him (a point which an agitated and disconsolate McEnroe made later on in the game), Connors took full advantage of his popularity. While McEnroe took helpless issue with the umpire over disputed points (almost chivalric in its pointlessness: to hell with right, might, fight and spite. The umpire had height on his side and sight, too) Connors took delight in accruing even more support. Waving his arms in 'What can a poor boy do?'

177

gestures, sitting amongst spectators to show he was just one of the guys and inviting McEnroe to the net for a chap to chap talk (thus, incidentally, breaking the rule that players do not communicate with each other during matches) and generally improvising a good guy act, he had the crowd in his palm for the latter part of the match.

It was, compared to the castigation McEnroe received for his misdemeanors, largely overlooked that he too had abused his racket, uttered audible obscenities, for which he was later fined, and disputed calls. Given a choice between McEnroe's petulance and Connors' knowing, cynical milking of public support (comparable to a disaster-prone, pedantically belligerent child and the school sneak), I found Connors' behaviour much more objectionable and unsportsmanlike.

Serving at love-1 and love-40 in the third set McEnroe suddenly smashed a ball into the back stop and was given a public warning. This seemed harsh as players often vent frustration by whacking balls away from the court like that. They are seldom penalised. In the ensuing argument with umpire John Parry, McEnroe hit the television microphone with his racket and was penalised a point. The grand prix supervisor was called and much of their violent argument was audible to both the crowd and television viewers. As the minutes passed the TV commentators, adopting a hand-wringing 'more in sorrow than in anger' tone, bewailed the degeneration of the match and the tragedy of McEnroe's temper. Connors smiled happily at his brother John in the stands, looked cheekily askance at the crowd, chatted to Earl Bucholz, executive director of the Association of Tennis Professionals, postured unashamedly and should have won an Oscar for his performance of wounded innocence. McEnroe's attempt to win back his penalised point had failed and the match resumed. Connors was revitalised and McEnroe as good as finished. There was futher abuse to officials from both McEnroe and Connors. When Connors beckoned Mac over to the net for a little chat, we presumed about getting on with the game, McEnroe shouted, 'Don't talk to me. You've got the crowd on your side and anything else you want.' The third set went to Connors 6-3.

Munching chocolate sadly between games and visibly upset, McEnroe fought on. There was remarkable tennis and every game was closely fought, but Connors took the fourth set in menacing form, 6-4. Early in the fifth set Mac fell and hurt his ankle but recovered and for a while seemed to be back in the match. But after failing to go 3-1 up although he had two break points in the fourth game, McEnroe then lost his own service. He hit a ball into the stands and was awarded yet another penalty. After this McEnroe took only a handful more points from Connors for the rest of the match. He looked incredibly depressed and Connors raced home with the final set 6-2. It put Connors 9-6 ahead in their match rivalry, but this time it had been McEnroe's professional suicide in the third set that had rekindled a flagging Connors and virtually given him the match.

Just before it was all over McEnroe had done something extraordinary: he smiled.

Afterwards he said, 'The umpire really screwed it up. I had not really done anything. When I hit the microphone with my racket all I did was break the strings. It was really stupid.' It lost him the will to win the match. A bad day altogether at Wembley, for he and Fleming lost the doubles final too, to Sherwood Stewart and Ferdi Taygan, 7-5, 6-7, 6-4.

The furore after the match was almost equal to the Wimbledon fuss. Connors, who had also been fined $400 for obscenities admitted that the crowd had baited McEnroe and that the rules were too restrictive. However he said he thought such a match had its advantages because it packed the halls, brought interest and controversy back into the game and produced good, aggressive tennis. McEnroe's two $350 fines, for racket and ball abuse, guaranteed his suspension. Since, he had no grand prix commitments for the next 21 days, this suited him fine. But clearly he took exception to the principle and guardedly alluded to the punishments that were metered out to him as compared with Connors. 'I have never been fined for anything obscene. Tennis is a great sport. You can't suppress personalities; you don't want robots on court. And conversations between the players and the referee should be private.'

Of the crowd who had stomped, jeered, heckled and

slow-handclapped at times Connors said, 'I guess they think they are New Yorkers. I like it better this way.'

Explaining his decision not to fight the ban McEnroe said, 'If I thought the pro council were human beings that would be fine, but they do not listen to any kind of reason. I do not understand how it all started. I just hit the ball into the back. I didn't think anything about it and the umpire's reaction surprised me.'

The umpiring had not generally been considered of the highest standard. Schoolmaster John Parry, in the hot seat, had been called stupid and lousy by McEnroe. Certainly he stumbled over the score several times and did not always seem to be in complete control. He said afterwards that he wasn't happy with his performance but that he stood by his decisions. He would like, he said, to umpire another McEnroe match. 'It wasn't one of my best days,' he said. While dicey officiating explains to some extent the players' reactions it does not excuse bad sportsmanship, and in this Connors and McEnroe shared equal dishonour that day.

But it should not be forgotten that they produced a rivetting match and three and a half hours of some of the most rhapsodic imaginative, and breath-taking finals that Wembley had seen. Soon afterwards McEnroe appeared on the cover of *Private Eye* and in the bubble coming from his mouth attributed his troubles to pre-menstrual tension. Rather a cheap laugh, and the following issue a spirited defence of Mac appeared in the letters column. The writer pointed out that Mac was now back on his winning streak, including a win in Spain.

Mournful admonitions about McEnroe's behaviour from TV reporters and accusations that he tries to intimidate line judges almost outweighed any attention given to the quality of the game afterwards. McEnroe is quite bright enough to know that his protests rarely intimidate anyone; he is likely to be the first to notice this. The Benson and Hedges furies were more likely, as usual, misguided emotional over-reaction. He is certainly adequately punished for his facial and verbal grumpiness. Small wonder then that, isolated and abused as he feels, he becomes even more distressed, only to be readily (sometimes eagerly), misunderstood. I wish they'd all lay off him for a bit.

The ban did not prevent McEnroe from competing in the final of the Davis Cup against Argentina with the U S team in Cincinnatti, in December 1981. He played magnificently in both the singles and the doubles and since Connors was unable to take part, hopes for the U S victory rested firmly with Mac. There was much audience disruption in those matches but also huge patriotic support for McEnroe who had found a stunning return to form. When he beat Jose-Luis Clerc in the match that decided the outcome of the series people wept and he was mobbed. The Cincinnatti Kid for a while and a good omen, perhaps, for his standing in 1982.

11

APOCALYPSE SOON OR THE SWINE IN SHORT PANTS

John McEnroe is now in a box. I hope no-one forgets to let him out when his detention is over
  Barry Newcombe, New Standard

You're doing a lousy job*

I have never been fined for anything obscene*

I swear that I'm a good guy*

McEnroe has not only degenerated the game of tennis. He has betrayed his country   *Letter in World Tennis*

The umpires are out to get me. They want to prove they can handle the big man*

Even the piss-ups are run-of-the-mill these days   *British journalist of tennis establishment cocktail party*

McEnroe is a meticulous player and demands the highest standards from the officials   *John Parry*

Those who consider that McEnroe has brought
the game into disrepute should consider that
over the years greed, allied to timid, vacillating
administration has already brought the game
into disrepute *Ronald Atkin, Observer*

My biggest ambition is to beat Borg on clay. I
want to beat him in three sets out of five on
clay, in Paris*

You have to roll with the punches. It's a lot harder that way but I'm a fighter, so I give it a try*

It's a lot harder to stay on top than to get
there*

I would be happy with myself if I thought I'd
given something back to the game*

John McEnroe

Summer 1982 and Wimbledon approaches. What can
we expect? We can expect bad weather, cold, rain and some
late starts. We can expect hours of 'bonk, bonk, 40-30,' on
the television and a couple of forests in Sweden will be cut
down to accommodate all the newsprint. We can expect a
new moppet from America to stun us with her precocious
tennis skills. We can expect some early sensations, when a
few of the seeds are knocked out by old lags or newcomers
from Eastern Europe or South America. There will be
champing at the bit and biting at the champ.

We can expect the usual number of complaints from
outraged schoolgirls about 'interference' from gentlemen in
the crowd. Elderly officials have been prosecuted in the past
and three years ago there was such a complaint against one of
the highest clergymen in the land. Penalty point for Wimbledon here in its moral crusade and love of propriety. We can

expect John McEnroe to promise to clean up his act. We may find, as usual, that injury or early defeat has jinxed him from doing well at the French Open, just as Borg is doomed at Flushing Meadow. We can expect a massive publicity build up about the expected Borg McEnroe final confrontation. We'll all be hoping they meet again on Saturday July 3rd on Centre Court. John McEnroe will probably be seen dining somewhere swanky like San Lorenzo with a girl who may or may not be Stacy Margolin . . . There will be prophesies that he is a burnt-out case. After defeats early in 1982 at the hands of Ivan Lendl and Johan Kriele, they had begun already.

Of course Borg may have a harder time of it this year. The international Tennis Federation specifies that to maintain their pro-status the players must take part in at least ten circuit events a year, as well as the big championships. Never one to overdo it, Borg's count is especially low this year because his wife's ill-health has kept him at home. If he hasn't competed in enough tournaments Borg will have to 'qualify' for Wimbledon. Like Mac in 1977, he'll have to play three matches at Roehampton before the championships proper.

Something else is new. This year for the first time some tickets for Centre Court will be made available by ballot during the last four days. This means that anyone has a chance of watching the semis or the finals even if they aren't lucky or well connected enough to have acquired tickets in advance. There's an innovation for Wimbledon.

John McEnroe will be there for the sixth time, but will he still be using the Dunlop Maxply (priced at around £50) or will he be wielding that new racket he's been talking about designing in America? Will there be a talented new boy with a foul mouth? Will a British player get beyond the second round? Will Mac have undergone a metamorphosis and be more like his hero Rod Laver, more in control and nicer to know? Does the public really want this? Will Bjorn roar through the qualifying rounds and through the championships to take back the title? Is McEnroe a one-year wonder champion?

Perhaps he will have made that pop record for Elton

John. It will be interesting to see if the near-inevitable McEnroe gimmick pop record, featuring boos, hisses 'Play on Mr. McEnroe' in a well-bred voice and Bronxish whinings from the singer, will be roaring up the charts too. Any satirical McEnroe take-off should strike the note in Positively Fourth Street when Dylan sneers, 'You'll know what a drag it is to see you.' I wouldn't mind betting that McEnroe's own record would be better. The clown that wants to play Hamlet. The small time offender who always meant to go straight. The boy who always wanted to play tennis. The great recidivist of the game.

There will be service without a smile. He probably will throw the tantrum and jump to conclusions. I hope to see him and Borg together in the final, not especially because I have any objection to Jimmy or Ivan or Vitas or Roscoe reaching the last two, but because I want Mac to prove that last year wasn't a fluke. Unfortunately I think this may be necessary for his credence as Wimbledon champion. And will McEnroe, if he wins, finally be invited to become an honorary member of the All England Lawn Tennis and Croquet Club? And if he does will he evoke the Groucho Marx Amendment: 'I do not wish to be associated with any club which will have me as a member'?

Almost certainly he will have a few words with a few officials at the Stella Artois tournament at Queens. It's early days yet, but he may find that people are less outraged by his remarks. There's plenty of time for another swing in popular opinion but after the Davis Cup final against Argentina McEnroe got popular for a while. He was 'Mac' in the papers, not 'Superbrat' after his 6-3, 6-2, 6-2 win over Vilas and the stupendous 7-5, 5-7, 6-3, 3-6, 6-3 match with Jose-Luis Clerc—which took over four hours. People cried and he was the hero who had done more than anyone else to retain the Cup for America in that North v South of the border confrontation.

Who knows how long such benign attention will last? Anyone can change and McEnroe may have more room for improvement than most. I wouldn't like to put money on an affable Mac instead of the dear familiar hooligan. But I hope that one day, one year, everyone will think it was all a bit of a joke. When it has been proved that McEnroe did not cause rapid moral decay amongst youngsters in the British Isles, when he has shown that he can play thunderingly beautiful tennis without getting into a tizz with himself or his opponent. When Dan Maskell, commenting on some cheeky newcomer will say, 'Well, in his early days even John McEnroe was regarded as a bit rough, wasn't he Mark?', when he's back to defend his title for the sixth successive year and he wins . . . maybe then we can all have a bit of a laugh about it, and say 'super, brat'.

'H' AUTOBIOGRAPHY OF A CHILD PROSTITUTE AND HEROIN ADDICT.

CHRISTIANE F.

The harrowing tragic exposé of young lives shattered. The most shocking account of young people caught up in the dark world of drug abuse since GO ASK ALICE (also available from Corgi Books)

NOW FILMED AS CHRISTIANE F.

0 552 11899 0   £1.50

HOVEL IN THE HILLS BY ELIZABETH WEST

This is the unsentimental, amusing, and absorbing account of the 'simple life' as practised by Alan and Elizabeth West in their primitive cottage in rural Wales. The Wests – she is a typist, he an engineer – moved from Bristol to North Wales in 1965, determined to leave the rat race for good. But the daunting task of converting a semi-derelict farmhouse and turning the unproductive soil into a viable self-sufficient unit was to prove a full-time job. The author describes the very individual and resourceful ways she and her husband tackled the problems which faced them – from slating the roof, curing a smoking chimney and generating their own electricity, growing a wonderful variety of fruit, herbs and vegetables on impossible soil. With a preface by John Seymour, author of 'The Complete Book of Self-Sufficiency', 'Hovel in the Hills' is a heartwarming and salutary tale which will either leave you yearning for a chance to get away from it all or convince you that the comfortable security of the nine-to-five is not such a bad thing.

0 552 10907 X   £1.25

GO ASK ALICE BY ANONYMOUS

Alice is fifteen, white, middle-class. She diets. She dates. She gets decent grades. She thinks someday she'd like to get married and raise a family.

On July 9, Alice is turned on to acid. She digs it. Acid makes the world a better place. So do all the other ups. They open up the world of sex. They make Alice feel free. Sometimes Alice worries about taking drugs. She thinks maybe she shouldn't. But, she figures life is more bearable with drugs than without.

Alice's parents don't know what's happening. They notice changes. They have no idea she's on drugs. They cannot help her.

The difference between Alice and a lot of other kids on drugs is that Alice kept a diary.

0 552 09332 7   £1.25

I'M DANCING AS FAST AS I CAN
BY BARBARA GORDON

'As chilling as One Flew Over The Cuckoo's Nest' – *Woman's World*

The intimate account of a woman
who found the courage to mend
her own shattered life

Barbara Gordon, a TV producer at the height of her career, had just been nominated for her third Emmy Award. But little did she know that, on the night of the awards ceremony she would be confined in a mental institution ...

   I'M DANCING AS FAST AS I CAN is Barbara's own story of the harrowing events that drove her to commit herself to a hospital as a mental patient – of the psychiatrist who failed her, of her agonizing 'cold turkey' withdrawal from tranquilizers – and of the lover who, when she needed him most, became not her ally but her enemy.

'Makes horrifying reading' – *Evening News*

'An unnerving book, an autobiography that reads compellingly like a novel' – *Oxford Mail*

'Gripping, provocative reading' – *Time Out*

'There's a warning for us all in this book' – *Company Magazine*

0 553 17729 X   £1.50

A SELECTED LIST OF AUTOBIOGRAPHIES, BIOGRAPHIES PUBLISHED BY CORGI

WHILE EVERY EFFORT IS MADE TO KEEP PRICES LOW, IT IS SOMETIMES NECESSARY TO INCREASE PRICES AT SHORT NOTICE. CORGI BOOKS RESERVE THE RIGHT TO SHOW AND CHARGE NEW RETAIL PRICES ON COVERS WHICH MAY DIFFER FROM THOSE ADVERTISED IN THE TEXT OR ELSEWHERE.

THE PRICES SHOWN BELOW WERE CORRECT AT THE TIME OF GOING TO PRESS (APRIL '82)

All these books are available at your bookshop or newsagent, or can be ordered direct from the publisher. Just tick the titles you want and fill in the form below.